CONFLICT & POWER IN MARRIAGE

SAGE LIBRARY OF SOCIAL RESEARCH

1. **David Caplovitz:**
   The Merchants of Harlem
2. **James N. Rosenau:**
   International Studies and the Social Sciences
3. **Douglas E. Ashford:**
   Ideology and Participation
4. **Patrick J. McGowan and Howard B. Shapiro:**
   The Comparative Study of Foreign Policy
5. **George A. Male:**
   The Struggle for Power
6. **Raymond Tanter:**
   Modelling and Managing International Conflicts
7. **Anthony James Catanese:**
   Planners and Local Politics
8. **James Russell Prescott:**
   Economic Aspects of Public Housing
9. **F. Parkinson:**
   Latin America, the Cold War, and the World Powers, 1945-1973
10. **Robert G. Smith:**
    Ad Hoc Governments
11. **Ronald Gallimore, Joan Whitehorn Boggs, and Cathie Jordan:**
    Culture, Behavior and Education
12. **Howard W. Hallman:**
    Neighborhood Government in a Metropolitan Setting
13. **Richard J. Gelles:**
    The Violent Home
14. **Jerry L. Weaver:**
    Conflict and Control in Health Care Administration
15. **Gebhard Ludwig Schweigler:**
    National Consciousness in Divided Germany
16. **James T. Carey:**
    Sociology and Public Affairs
17. **Edward W. Lehman:**
    Coordinating Health Care
18. **Charles G. Bell and Charles M. Price:**
    The First Term
19. **Clayton P. Alderfer and L. Dave Brown:**
    Learning from Changing
20. **L. Edward Wells and Gerald Marwell:**
    Self-Esteem
21. **Robert S. Robins:**
    Political Institutionalization and the Integration of Elites
22. **William R. Schonfeld:**
    Obedience and Revolt
23. **William C. McCready and Andrew M. Greeley:**
    The Ultimate Values of the American Population
24. **F. Ivan Nye:**
    Role Structure and Analysis of the Family
25. **Paul Wehr and Michael Washburn:**
    Peace and World Order Systems
26. **Patricia R. Stewart:**
    Children in Distress
27. **Juergen Dedring:**
    Recent Advances in Peace and Conflict Research
28. **Moshe M. Czudnowski:**
    Comparing Political Behavior
29. **Jack D. Douglas:**
    Investigative Social Research
30. **Michael Stohl:**
    War and Domestic Political Violence
31. **Nancy E. Williamson:**
    Sons or Daughters
32. **Werner Levi:**
    Law and Politics in the International Society
33. **David L. Altheide:**
    Creating Reality
34. **Allan Lerner:**
    The Politics of Decision-Making
35. **Philip E. Converse:**
    The Dynamics of Party Support
36. **Charles L. Newman and Barbara R. Price:**
    Jails and Drug Treatment
37. **Clarence L. Abercrombie III:**
    The Military Chaplain
38. **Mark Gottdiener:**
    Planned Sprawl
39. **Robert L. Lineberry:**
    Equality and Urban Policy
40. **Patrick M. Morgan:**
    Deterrence
41. **Vladimir A. Lefebvre:**
    The Structure of Awareness
42. **Andrea Fontana:**
    The Last Frontier
43. **Robert V. Kemper:**
    Migration and Adaptation
44. **David Caplovitz and Fred Sherrow:**
    The Religious Drop-Outs
45. **Stuart S. Nagel and Marian Neef:**
    The Legal Process: Modeling the System
46. **Rue Bucher and Joan G. Stelling:**
    Becoming Professional
47. **Paul Hiniker:**
    Revolutionary Ideology and Chinese Reality
48. **Simon N. Herman:**
    Jewish Identity
49. **Alan Marsh:**
    Protest and Political Consciousness
50. **Ralph LaRossa:**
    Conflict and Power in Marriage
51. **Bengt Abrahamsson:**
    Bureaucracy or Participation
52. **F. Parkinson:**
    The Philosophy of International Relations

CONFLICT & POWER IN MARRIAGE:
EXPECTING THE FIRST CHILD

Ralph LaRossa

A SageMark Edition

SAGE Publications / Beverly Hills / London

Copyright © 1977 by Sage Publications, Inc.

For information address:

SAGE PUBLICATIONS, INC.
275 South Beverly Drive
Beverly Hills, California 90212

SAGE PUBLICATIONS LTD
28 Banner Street
London EC1Y 8QE

Printed in the United States of America

Library of Congress Cataloging in Publication Data

LaRossa, Ralph.
   Conflict and power in marriage.

   (Sage library of social research ; v. 50)
   Includes index.
   1. Family—United States. 2. Married people—
Interviews. 3. Pregnancy—Psychological aspects.
I. Title.
HQ536.L37   301.42'7   77-8566
ISBN 0-8039-0878-4
ISBN 0-8039-0879-2 pbk.

FIRST SAGEMARK PRINTING, SPRING 1979

To Maureen

CONTENTS

Chapter   *Page*

Preface by Murray A. Straus   9

Acknowledgments   13

Cast of Characters   15

1. Introduction   17

2. Daryl and Debby   33

3. Hank and Helen   51

4. Joe and Jennifer   69

5. Lloyd and Linda   83

6. A Conflict Approach to Marriage: Presuppositions   103

7. A Conflict Approach to Marriage: The Problem
    of Social Order   125

8. Epilogue   149

Appendix   153

References   159

Author Index   163

Subject Index   165

About the Author   171

PREFACE

A holistic, processual approach to the study of the family (or almost anything else) is probably the approach preferred by most sociologists. Graduate students I have worked with over the years typically enter the program with such a perspective. It is usually expressed in the form of a preference for qualitative rather than quantitative research methods. This preference is based on a sound (but often inarticulate) understanding of the fact that the heart of sociological analysis is the interpretation of social processes, purposive acts, and the structure of relationships which emerges from these interactions. But few of these students end up with a dissertation reflecting these theoretical and methodological preferences. What accounts for the difference between what enters the graduate student pipeline and what emerges five years later? There are several possible explanations.

The first is what might be called a power or brainwashing explanation. This explanation assumes that graduate departments of sociology (or at least the influential faculty) are analytical rather than holistic in their conception of sociology. These faculty, by virtue of their control of the curriculum and of dissertation committees, brainwash or coerce students away from a holistic perspective.

I must say that this is not my perception of things. Except for the minority of faculty who teach statistics and methods (and not even all of those), most of the sociologists I have been associated with are closer to a "holistic" than to an "analytic" approach in their *beliefs* about the nature of society and the best way of finding out about the nature of human society. But, like the students they teach, those who do empirical research most often end up employing a static, analytical, quantitative approach. So it seems that something similar to what goes on during the training of graduate students also occurs among the faculty.

Now we have two puzzles to unravel! If one takes the brainwashing explanation for the graduate student puzzle, then one must also ask who is brainwashing or coercing the faculty away from doing research which is consistent with their beliefs? Why do so many of us profess to have a holistic approach, but publish work which can better be described as falling within the analytical side of the categories used by LaRossa to describe his research?

Those committed to the brainwashing or power explanation will not long search for words. Indeed, many such words are to be found in the letters to the editors section of our journals, and especially in the *American Sociologist* and in *Footnotes*: We can call this the "establishment journal" explanation. It is a conspiracy theory which holds that the editors and editorial boards who decide on what is to be published favor analytic and quantitative papers. As a result, what qualitative research is done seldom gets published. This, in turn, steers sociologists to do the kind of research which will be more favorably reviewed. Again, I must say that, attractive as this theory is, it does not square with my experience as the editor of a journal and member of the editorial board of other journals. The editorial policy of each of these journals has been one of encouraging articles which fall within the holistic approach.

The explanation which I suggest as the primary basis for the dominance of the analytical over the holistic in the sociological research is that holistic research is extremely difficult to carry out. First, the technical problems connected with a quantitative approach to holistic analysis are extreme. So one must depend on nonquantitative research to get at what

are probably the most central issues in furthering our understanding of the family. But that only makes the problem
more difficult because, contrary to what many think, qualitative research is probably something that a smaller proportion of sociologists know how to do well, or can be trained
to do well, than quantitative research. All science—quantitative or qualitative, physical, biological, or social—is partly
an art form, demanding creativity and certain esthetic judg-
ments. This is particularly true of qualitative research in
sociology. Not everyone is capable of producing works of
art of this type. Many of us have tried and failed. Others have
tried, and not knowing that they have failed, sent in articles
for publication, only to have them rejected. There are many
things which make qualitative research such as that reported
in this book difficult. I will mention only two.

First is the fact that, in qualitative as well as quantitative
research, empirical evidence is needed. In quantitative research the evidence is represented by such things as percent-
ages, averages, correlations, etc. Whether these statistics are
believable or not depends, in part, on the test of significance
which tells the reader what the likelihood is that these results
could have occurred just by chance. So, if a researcher reports
a correlation between the number of months married and the
husbands power of .38 which is significant at the .001 level,
the reader knows that there is a tendency for the husbands
power to increase during the early years of marriage. In addition, a result like the one reported is believable in the sense
that the probability of getting a finding like this by chance
alone is less than one in a thousand. But if the researcher is
doing a qualitative study of 10 or 15 families and reports that
the longer the couple had been married, the higher the husband's power, why should we believe him or her? In fact, it
is not very believable because that is a conclusion for which
evidence is needed. Herein lies the first difficulty. In qualitative research the investigator must report the events which
led to this conclusion, and must report them in a way which
enables the reader to partly relive the experience of the peo-

ple studied. The reader, like the researcher, then "knows" that the generalization is correct. Unfortunately, this requires more than just voluminous field notes. It is, as I said, an art form, and not all of us have the ability to produce such works of art.

The second difficulty standing in the way of more widespread use of the methodology represented by this book is the fact that, although a rich description of ongoing emergent social processes is essential, it is not sufficient. The classic field studies are all characterized by this living description. They are also characterized by being the basis for developing, testing, or refining a theory. This is difficult to achieve, but even more damaging is the fact that many of those setting out to do holistic studies do not realize that without theory there is no sociology. They tend to confuse a holistic approach with a purely descriptive approach.

Fortunately, there are some sociologists who do have the skills and the concern for theory needed to overcome these and other barriers to holistic research. Ralph LaRossa is one of them. His book enlightens as to the particulars and the general theoretical principles underlying conflict and power in marriage.

May 11, 1977   *Murray A. Straus*
Durham, New Hampshire

ACKNOWLEDGMENTS

My good friend and colleague Howard M. Shapiro furnished the stimulus for this venture into the marital experience. He convinced me to do an in-depth study of married couples. He also served as an advisor and critic throughout the project. I am deeply grateful for his inspiration and support.

Murray A. Straus, Jetse Sprey, Bonnie Mintz Cooper, Loren Cobb, Raymond L. Erickson, and Lance Kirkpatrick Canon all refused to be easily impressed and made recommendations which led to substantive revisions. Their efforts are very much appreciated.

There would be no study were it not for the sample couples. I am indebted to them all. My promise, however, to protect their identities prevents me from naming them or the health care professionals who introduced me to them.

Kent Allyn, Eileen O'Grady, and Susan Rhoades transcribed the interview tapes. Anne Kohl, Elaine Marsh, and Jim Wilson typed the manuscript in its various stages.

This study was funded in part by a grant from the University of New Hampshire research fund.

A special thanks is due to my parents for their confidence and encouragement.

Finally, I want to acknowledge the contribution of my wife Maureen. She, too, refused to be easily impressed and made suggestions which led to substantive revisions. But, more importantly, her selflessness during some rather difficult times made possible the completion of this book. When I really needed her, she was there.

Ralph LaRossa

CAST OF CHARACTERS

Alan and Amy
Brad and Barbara
Carl and Cheryl
Daryl and Debby
Eric and Elizabeth
Fitz and Fran
George and Gloria
Hank and Helen
Ike and Irene
Joe and Jennifer
Kevin and Karen
Lloyd and Linda
Mark and Marie
Norman and Nancy
Owen and Olyvia
Peter and Pam

Chapter 1

INTRODUCTION

Based on conjoint, in-depth interviews with sixteen couples expecting their first child, this book is manifestly a study of how husbands and wives respond to the first pregnancy. At a higher level of abstraction, however, and more importantly, it is a close-up examination of the marital system.

Two Studies in One

A STUDY OF FIRST PREGNANCY

Although medical (physiological) and psychological monographs and papers on pregnant women abound, there are few studies which deal with (a) the effect of the first pregnancy on the marital relationship, or (b) the effect of the marital relationship on the husband and/or wife's first pregnancy experiences. The reasons why the social linkage between marriage and pregnancy has been neglected are not hard to come by. Traditionally, the male's role in the birth process has been viewed as "getting the job done" (as one of the husbands in the sample put it) and then "letting nature take its course." Given this attitude, it is understandable why expectant fathers have been ignored by researchers. Given this attitude, it is also understandable why the literature on the nonmedical aspects of pregnancy is dominated by studies of "nonnormal," "deviant," or "problem" pregnancies (Miller, 1973). Very much a part of the idea that birth is "a woman's thing" is the feeling that childbrearing is "natural" for women and that pregnancy is essentially a continuation and extension of the female role (Stewart and Erickson, 1976). From this point of view, the only nonmedical issues deemed worthy of study are those which are supposedly at odds with "the natural progression of events"—for example, premarital pregnancy.

It is absurd, however, to suggest that pregnancy is too "natural" to be of any concern to social scientists. Being female may be a necessary prerequisite to motherhood, but it is not the sufficient condition. Essentially, the idea that pregnancy is "natural" for women presumes that the only role which is, and should be, available to women is the parental role. The number of women in the labor force belies this notion. Speaking of working women, the increased number of employed wives raises a more important point. Evidence suggests that because of the incompatibility of occupational with parental roles in our society, career-oriented people may be more likely to view the first pregnancy as a negative experience (McCorkel, 1964). With more and more wives pursuing careers, might we hypothesize that, other things being equal, everyday, "normal" first pregnancy will increasingly mean more stress for women?

It is also absurd to believe that pregnancy does not affect marriage, that it affects only the wife. With the advent of more efficient contraceptives, husbands and wives are now able to develop their marital roles in the absence of children. Many couples in fact are waiting several years before they start a family. Given that couples are more "set in their ways" at conception, the first pregnancy now means more of a shift in routine than before. Furthermore, studies dividing subjects by marital type indicate that companionship-type marriages are more likely to be negatively affected by the transition to parenthood (Feldman, 1974). These couples tend to worry more about whether the child will interfere with their relationships. Since marriage as an institution is becoming more and more a companionship arrangement, might we offer another hypothesis to complement the first: that, other things being equal, the first pregnancy will increasingly become a crisis for the marital system?

In sum, one justification for this book is the growing need for research on the social linkage between the first pregnancy and the husband-wife relationship.

A STUDY OF MARRIAGE

As significant as the transition to parenthood is, the primary reason I undertook this research is that I wanted to conduct a qualitative study of "normal" middle-class American marriages.[1] Despite the importance of the husband-wife relationship in American society (no other role relationship is more central or more valued), we actually know very little about the American conjugal experience. How can this be true with so many "experts" surveying the American marital scene? The problem is two-fold. First, the most popular tools of the family researcher—the mailed questionnaire and the structured interview—are of limited value if one is interested in gaining an in-depth understanding of the married state. Both strategies fail in that they force upon the couple the researcher's preconceived system of meanings rather than permit the couple's patterns to emerge. Second, many of the studies which attempt to deal with this problem by using multiple unstructured interviews or home observations prove also to be limited because they rely to a large degree either on clinical families (e.g., Henry, 1965), the elite (e.g., Cuber and Harroff, 1965), or blue collar samples (e.g., Howell, 1973; Komarovsky, 1962), or they focus for the most part on the

parent-child relationship rather than the husband-wife relationship (e.g., Hess and Handel, 1959; Kantor and Lehr,
1975).

You may be wondering why, if I was primarily interested
in studying the American marital experience, I chose to interview such a select group myself.

In order to do more than scratch the surface of a couple's
life it is necessary to gain entrance not only into their home,
but into their private world as well (Hill, 1949). Pregnancy
provided an intermediary (obstetrical group practices)
through which I could "get in the door." And the transition
to parenthood provided an issue which would make the couples' marriages more transparent to me. The assumption I
was making is that social systems are less opaque during
change. This is not a new idea but is generally recognized by
researchers. For example, in the opening chapter of his an-
thropology of poverty, Oscar Lewis outlines the approaches
he used during his many years of studying Mexican families.
One of his techniques speaks directly to this point (Lewis,
1959: 4): "Select for intensive study a problem or a special
event or a crisis to which the family reacts. The way a family
meets new situations is revealing of many latent aspects of
family psychodynamics; it also points up individual differences." And of course the technique of "disturbing the
scene" to uncover "the routine grounds of everyday life,"
popular among ethnomethodologists (Garfinkel, 1967), implies a similar strategy. Thus, the reason expectant couples
were chosen for this study of marriage is that through their
reactions to impending parenthood, I would be able to make
some inroads into the carefully guarded marital world.[2]

Marriage as an Emergent System

There are basically two approaches in science—the analytical approach and the holistic approach. Whereas the analytical
approach emphasizes the division of entities into constituent
elements, for example, into independent and dependent vari-

ables, the holistic approach, as the name implies, emphasizes an examination of the totality—"taking it all together, how does the whole thing work?" (Weiss, 1966: 200). The approach taken in this book is holistic.

The most important assumption made by the holistically oriented investigator is that a system is emergent—it is more than the sum of its parts. The significance of this principle for the family researcher is noted by Watzlawick and his colleagues (1967: 134-139):

> Formal analysis of [a system's] artifically isolated segments would destroy the very object of interest. It is necessary to neglect the parts for the gestalt and attend to the core of its complexity, its organization. . . . The analysis of a family is [therefore] not the sum of its individual members. There are characteristics of the system . . . that transcend the qualities of individual members.

Given this conceptual approach and the qualitative methodological stance noted previously, it should be understandable that there will be no formal hypotheses presented. Rather, only the two general questions which have guided this inquiry shall be specified:

(1) How does the husband-wife system work during the first pregnancy?

(2) How does the husband-wife system work in general?

Methodology

THE COUPLES

Getting couples for the study involved a number of steps: First, I sought the help of friends and contacts who were themselves associated with the medical profession. The suggestions of these people resulted in the drafting of a letter which was subsequently mailed to target persons, mostly obstetricians, in four medical groups: one prenatal clinic,

one family planning agency, and two obstetrical team practices. Each letter was followed up with a phone call in which
I asked to meet personally with representatives from each of
the groups. The first week after the letters were mailed, I
talked with the supervisors of the prenatal clinic and family
planning agency. Both agreed to help in any way they could.
They informed me, however, that they could not guarantee
many referrals because their clients were unlikely to come to
them during the first quarter of the pregnancy (which is
when I wanted to conduct the first of four interviews). For
the prenatal clinic (a free clinic servicing the less privileged)
it was too early. Lower-class women tend to wait until the
second and sometimes the third quarter to confirm that they
are pregnant. For the family planning agency the first quarter
was too late. They primarily provided a service for women
who did not want to get pregnant; if they did, they rarely
told the agency. Having first met with these two groups, I
knew that the success of the study depended on the cooperation of the obstetricians. My original plan was to ask
the doctors whether they would be willing to furnish the
names of primiparous women to whom I would then mail
letters, addressed to both the husband and wife, introducing
myself and the project. When I met with the doctors, they
suggested that they or their nurses personally hand the letters to the women and that I be presented with the recipients'
names and phone numbers. I could then call and ask if the
couple had made their decision whether or not to participate.
The obstetricians felt that a direct endorsement from them
would increase the chances of a high acceptance rate. This
procedure was put into effect.

In the beginning I intended to include twenty couples in
the sample. Based on the estimates of how many first-time
pregnant women the two groups would see over the next two
months (the time interval calculated, given my time limitations), I decided not to be selective in my sampling. With the
exception that all who were approached were primiparous
women whose babies were due within a specified time frame,

the sampling procedure was "accidental" (Selltiz et al., 1976: 517). During the two-month interval, twenty-eight couples were referred. The two obstetrical groups each provided thirteen names. The prenatal clinic and family planning agency each furnished one. The sixteen couples who ultimately agreed to participate thus constitute 57 percent of the couples contacted.[3] With the exception that the husbands and wives were all white residents of towns and small cities in New England, the sixteen couples, when compared across other demographic characteristics, proved to be quite diverse (see Appendix).

It is often useful to know what motivates people to accept or reject a request to be in a study. When I called a couple, if they did not want to participate, I would try to find out why. The reasons given varied. One wife said they were moving out of the state, that if they were not, they would have been glad to be in the study. Two wives claimed that their husbands worked days and evenings, that it would just be "too much." In a few cases, I received the impression that the wife wanted to participate but the husband did not. In two cases this was made explicit. One wife said that they felt the pregnancy was "a personal thing" and that they wanted to keep it that way. For half of the nonparticipants I was unable to get any specific reasons. This was due, in part, to my not forcing the issue. I did not want to disrupt the doctor-patient relationship.

The reasons couples decided to participate also varied. First of all, there was the endorsement from the medical groups. Many of the couples who opted to be in the study would not have done so were it not for my association with the doctors. As one husband put it:

PETER: We had faith in the doctor, and if he recommends you it kind of takes the tension away.

Some couples wanted it made "perfectly clear" that they were not in the study for their own benefit but for mine. For example:

BARBARA: We're pretty comfortable with the pregnancy, and we don't feel that we have to use you for getting our own thrills out of this whole thing. I think we look more towards being of help to you.

But then some other couples admitted that they were in it for themselves too.

CARL: The reason why we decided to do it was so that I could communicate more with Cheryl. Because she tells me almost everything, but if I have a bad day at work, I come home and slam the door.

ELIZABETH: Another motivation for helping you out in this study is that it focuses some of it for us too.

ERIC: As we're doing this, all these things, I'm kind of on the outside looking in and seeing how we can improve our marriage at the same time.

INTERVIEWER: Are you doing it for me or are you doing it for Linda?

LLOYD: For you and Linda.

LINDA: No, Well—

LLOYD: It started out for you [speaking to his wife].

LINDA: Yes, I guess it did start out for me.

THE INTERVIEWS

Other than a background questionnaire used to gather information on age, education, income, etc., the research was totally based on four conjoint (husband and wife together), conversational interviews.

The reason a relatively unstructured mode of interviewing was chosen was to gain as much of an internal perspective as possible. In other words, I wanted to minimize the extent to which the couple would have to translate their world into my boxes.

The nature of the phenomenon under study also guided me in the choice of the conjoint interview mode. An important part of the marital world is the mutually understood conceptions of the husband and wife. Interviews with only one of the parties in a marriage are insufficient for gaining access to these conceptions. For example, if only the wife is interviewed, instead of getting the couple's mutually understood conceptions—the husband and wife's conceptions of an object or situation and their conceptions of each other's conceptions—the researcher is actually getting the wife's view of her own and her husband's conceptions and her conception of their conceptions of each other's conceptions. Separate interviews with both the husband and wife are one means of gathering these data. This is essentially what Laing and his colleagues (1966) do with their interpersonal perception method. This method, however, relies on structured interviews. Consequently, the picture derived is somewhat shallow. If one does not want to restrict a couple's responses, which I did not, trying to infer mutually understood conceptions from separate interviews is, at best, difficult. Only in the conjoint interview can the interviewer play the husband and wife off against each other (e.g., "Were you aware of your husband's feelings on that? Were you aware of your wife's feelings about your feelings?"). An additional, though circumscribed, advantage of the conjoint interview is that the researcher also obtains a behavioral document of the couple's interactions.[4]

Mutiple interviews were chosen to permit me to gradually build a rapport with each couple. The premise was that the more contact I had with each couple, the more I would be able to get beyond the couple's shell. Comments made by the couples lend support to this assumption, for example:

CHERYL: I get the feeling, although I don't remember the first interview that much, there was a lot more of our trying to please you, trying to give you the picture of the happy couple, trying to describe ourselves in the way that maybe we would like to be, or something, whereas along the course of the interviews we've told

you the things we've argued about, and we certainly couldn't
have done that in the first interview right off the bat.

Multiple interviews also minimized the probability that a
couple could successfully present a facade. I assumed that I
could pick up most attempts to do so by cross-referencing
the couple's comments and then asking them about the in-
consistencies. Of course, inconsistency might be part of a
couple's world. If it was, I would still be more likely to pick
it up with multiple interviews.

Given that the research was to be a study of first pregnancy as well as a study of marriage, the interviews were scheduled around the physical reality of pregnancy. Each couple
would be interviewed four times during approximately the
twelfth, twentieth, twenty-eighth, and thirty-sixth week of the
pregnancy. Typically, a woman who suspects that she is pregnant will undergo a pregnancy test sometime around the
sixth week. I was told by the health care professionals, however, that I would probably not be able to conduct the first
interview until the twelfth week. The delay is a function of
(a) late pregnancy tests (many women wait until well after
the sixth week to make sure that their suspicions are not false
alarms); and (b) referral time (the time-lags between the
pregnancy test and my initial contact with the couples). While
it is true that by the twelfth week the physical cycle of pregnancy is almost one-third complete, it is still less than a
month, and often less than two weeks after the couple has
become aware of the pregnancy. Thus, by the twelfth week
the nonphysical cycle of pregnancy (the psycho-social dimension) is still in its early stages. The twentieth week was
chosen for the second interview because by this time most
women have experienced quickening—the first feeling of the
fetus in the uterus. By the twenty-eighth week, the wife has
acquired the shape of pregnancy. Her physical appearance
announces her condition. By conducting the fourth and final
interview four weeks before the couples' expected due dates,
the obvious problems which a premature delivery would pose

were minimized.[5] The thirty-sixth week is still close enough
to birth, however, to assess the couples' responses to immi-
nent parenthood.

All sixty-four interviews (16 x 4) were conducted by me
in the couples' homes. Most of the interviews were in the
evenings, but there were some on Saturday mornings. Each
interview lasted about an hour and a half, was taped, and
later transcribed.

ANALYSIS

In order to synthesize the interviews it was necessary to
develop from the transcripts a set of conceptual categories
across which the couples could be compared. To facilitate
the construction of these categories, I established a flexible
file consisting of selected passages cut from the transcripts
and pasted on 5 x 8 cards. Recognizing, first of all, that the
sooner the transcripts were cut up, the sooner I would ac-
quire a more rigid conceptual set toward the data, the flexible
file was not created until the interviews were just about
completed. Second, when I finally began cutting and pasting,
I opted for a more or less free flow method. Anything that
might be relevant was cut out. By the time I had gone once
through all the transcripts available to me at the time, I had
built an extensive pile (not file) of segregated passages. The
next step was to go through the pile and develop headings
under which specific passages might be legitimately placed.
In the beginning I found that each card seemed to imply a
different heading. Soon I came across cards that could be
grouped under established headings. However, before a card
would be filed with others, I would review the other cards in
the file to see how this passage fit.[6] I went through the transcripts again and again, each time cutting and carding more
passages. These succeeding runs were increasingly influenced
by the emergent category scheme which was being developed
as new cards became available for filing. By the time I fin-
ished, over sixteen hundred passages had been carded.

Preview

The heart of the book consists of a presentation of four of the sixteen couples in a case study format.[7] Each case study couple is followed (retrospectively) from before their marriage to and through (longitudinally) their first pregnancy. The level of analysis is a balance between the concrete and the abstract. Quotations from the couples give each case its depth. Substantive theories are integrated with the transcripts when their inclusion helps to explain a given sequence or event.

One question that is often raised when a case study format is used is the question of generalization: What can we learn about the general case from the specific cases studied? I personally believe that we can learn a great deal. As Hess and Handel (1959: ix) noted in their classic study of five families: "The detailed examination of cases suggests lines of thought, urges re-examination of contemporary theory, reveals areas of behavior in which our knowledge is sparse, and stimulates hypotheses that may be tested in other research formats." Somewhat more to the point are Weiss's (1966: 202) comments on the heuristic value of husband-wife case studies:

> In a study of the organization of a marriage . . . only material of the density available in the study of a single case—or a few cases—could support speculation that a complex balance is maintained in the marriage dependent on the continued presence of the girl's mother, the continued availability for the husband of a group of men with whom he had been friendly for years, a particular patterning of activities outside the home, a particular set of job demands, and particular expectations of marriage and of each other on the part of husband and wife. In a case approach there would be a wealth of anecdotal material bearing on the contribution of each element to the quality of the marriage. In addition, the couple themselves might appraise the role of various factors. If the case is followed over a period of time, there might be material describing the shift in the organization of the marriage coinciding with change in other factors. The repetition of incidents revealing information about a few interrelated themes—

in general, the density and focus of the data—enables the investigator to become fairly confident of the validity of a quite complex description of the case organization.

Some of the illustrations Weiss mentions in fact are exhibited
by the couples documented here. One couple's marriage and
transition to parenthood are greatly influenced by the actual
and implied presence of the wife's mother. Another couple's
"give and take" is centered around their work. Conflicting
definitions of the husband-wife relationship contribute to
major problems in one and minor skirmishes in another. All
of the couples, to varying degrees, show organizational shifts
over the course of the pregnancy.

What I have learned from the case studies as well as the
total sample comprises the last three chapters of the book.
After reading and rereading the sixteen hundred pages of
transcripts and trying to synthesize them into some coherent
framework, I have come to the conclusion that marriage in
general and marriage during first pregnancy in particular are
best understood from a conflict perspective. In other words,
rather than conceptualizing marriage as a consensus-equilibrium relationship, the conjugal dyad is best viewed as a system in which confrontation ("conflicts of interest") is inevitable and agreement problematic (Sprey, 1969: 702). The
conflict approach to social life has a long tradition, so this
conclusion is hardly new. Nevertheless, the idea that marriage
is a conflict system does contradict the popular conceptions.
The literature on the conflict approach to marriage has also
been essentially theoretical in scope; empirical support is
sorely lacking. This book therefore helps to bridge a research
gap. In fact, I would argue that the research reported here
constitutes the best available data on the conflict approach
to family life.

Before getting into the meat of the book, let me say again
that it is not the purpose of this research to isolate variables
and test hypotheses. Rather, it is my intent to describe, in
detail, four variations of a social form (marriage during its

transition to parenthood) and to generate from these descriptions, as well as from my notes on the other twelve couples, ideas about the nature of marriage and ideas about the nature of first pregnancy.[8] Given this, the breadth of the data (the degree to which they represent a specified population) is not as important as the depth of the data (the degree to which they cover the aspects of the phenomena in question). In this research, breadth has been sacrificed for depth. The result is a study which depicts the husband-wife relationship in "flesh-and-blood" terms.

NOTES

1. "Qualitative methodology refers to those research strategies such as participant observation, in-depth interviewing, total participation in the activity being investigated, field work, etc., which allow the researcher to . . . 'get close to the data,' thereby developing the analytical, conceptual, and categorical components of explanation from the data itself—rather than from the preconceived, rigidly structured, and highly quantified techniques that pigeonhole the empirical social world into operational definitions that the researcher has constructed" (Filstead, 1970: 6).

2. This is not the first study to use the first pregnancy as a medium to study marriage. See Olson (1969).

3. Given the degree of commitment being demanded from the couples, a 57% acceptance rate is rather good. For some reason, field researchers often neglect to mention acceptance rates. One of the few to do so is Bott (1971). Of the forty-five families contacted for that project, twenty-five (56%) were willing to be studied. Five of these, however, were rejected by the research team because they did not fit the study's criteria. Thus, only 44% of the families originally contacted ultimately participated.

4. The fact that the interactions have taken place in front of an interviewer requires that the researcher be critical of any inferences based on the behavioral data (Vidich, 1956). Recognizing this limitation, it is still noteworthy that the conjoint interview is the most popular clinical tool of the marital and family therapist (Olson, 1970) and that the opportunity to observe first-hand the couple's and/or family's interactions is one of the most often cited advantages of the method (see, for instance, Satir, 1964).

5. One couple in the sample did have their baby prematurely. Their fourth interview was conducted postpartum.

6. This strategy of each time comparing a new passage with the passages already grouped is akin to what Glaser and Strauss (1967: 101ff.) call the "constant comparative method."

7. Although the sample as a whole is relatively heterogeneous, the four case study husbands and wives, for the most part, are college educated professionals or executives. The homogeneity of the case study couples is due to the fact that the four were not chosen because they were representative of the sample; they were chosen because they were the couples for whom I had the most data (the largest sets of transcripts and the most notes). Of course, given the conversational interviews, the characteristics of the case study couples are not surprising. Any decision based on the depth of the data would more than likely be biased toward the more articulate couples.

8. For a discussion of how theory can be generated from qualitative research, see Glaser and Strauss (1967).

Chapter 2

DARYL AND DEBBY

When I wrote the first draft of this case study, I based my comments on the contention that for Daryl and Debby pregnancy and parenthood did not seem to be a crisis. I am using the term crisis in a very general sense to mean that in my view the couple did not see the event as a threat, a challenge, a call for new action, or a call for a change in plans.[1] One reason for my contention was that the decision of whether or not to have a child was not viewed by them as a major decision in their lives. Daryl and Debby went so far as to say that they felt they had put more thought into when to get their cat than they did into when to have a child. When I asked whether they had planned the pregnancy, I was first given the impression that they had used something of a laissez-faire approach (if it happens, it happens). Only after probing did I learn that Debby had intentionally stopped taking her birth control pills during the eighth month of their marriage and they supposed, if I wanted to categorize them, they would fall into the category of "planned pregnancy."

Debby offered her explanation of why her transition to motherhood was relatively crisis-free.

INTERVIEWER: Did you ever entertain the thought of not having children?

DEBBY: Me, seriously. Yes.

DARYL: Yes, that's right . . . what changed your mind, dear, about that? I know that it changed. We never really probed that situation.

DEBBY: It is probably because so many of our friends have adorable babies. . . . That had something to do with it I'm sure. Plus our relationship had something to do with it. When you're 22 or 23 and you're very independent and someone says, "Well don't you want to get married, settled down, and have kids," your first reaction is to tell them what they can do with it—"Go take a flying leap out the next highest window!" But I think after settling down and getting married, it just seemed like the logical thing to do!

Placing the blame on peer influence and "getting married" (taking on the role of wife) seemed sociopsychologically sound. One question remained, however. What happened during the first eight months of her marriage? In other words, what was it about "settling down and getting married" that prompted the revolution in her way of thinking? In order to answer this question, I was forced to look at Daryl and Debby's marriage chronologically. Seeing their relationship over time permitted me to recognize the changes in action and plans which the pregnancy had initiated and which parenthood would bring. Contrary to my earlier beliefs, pregnancy and parenthood were crises for the couple. The truth was that Daryl and Debby, throughout their marriage, had been engaged in a conflict of wills. Within this contest, having a baby was "the logical thing" for Debby to do because (a) Daryl had in effect left her no choice, and (b) the child would give her the means to launch an offensive.

Before her marriage, Debby was intent on carving out a career for herself. She had gone to college and had decided while there to become an elementary school teacher. She had had the opportunity to spend her junior year of college in Europe. Her grades and determination were sufficient to earn her a graduate teaching assistantship at the university where she received her bachelor's degree. As a graduate student she had the opportunity to teach her own freshman course in her specialty. She also was able to find a substitute teaching position at the local grammar school. It was while she was subing that her prejudice against having children crystallized.

DEBBY: It was always my idea that I didn't want to have children. Basically, I'm petrified of kids because I'm an only child and I'd never been around little boys and girls until I taught school and then I hated them even more.

Debby considered herself an "independent" person. She took particular pride in the fact that she was, from her point of view, not easily swayed by others, that she did, more or less, what she wanted to do and if people didn't like it, "tough!"

Daryl had been married before but had been divorced from his first wife for about seven years when he met Debby. He had one child by his previous marriage, but by the time he remarried, he was no longer responsible for alimony or child support. He had a bachelor's degree in engineering and worked for a local company. He thought of himself as something of a happy-go-lucky type; he enjoyed his work, but he enjoyed his play more. His spare time activities included ham radio competition[2] (his first love), golf, and working on his car, among other things. When he and Debby first got together, he was not working but was "taking off for the year." He implied that he was out of work by choice.

After knowing each other for a little over a year, they decided to get engaged. Nine months later they were married. The first six months of married life were rough. Each had come to the marriage with different conceptions of how a marriage should work. During one of the interviews, Debby offered what she believed to be the main reason for their different outlook on things.

DEBBY: He's a male chauvinist . . . because of his parents. In his entire life, I don't think his mother ever said "no" to anything his father or any of the kids wanted to do. . . . Whereas I'm just the opposite. I've watched my mother manipulate my father for years.

Of course, Debby's analysis is retrospective. It seems, so she claimed, that while they were dating, she had no idea that her marriage would be a relationship in which her role would be essentially that of Daryl's cook and housecleaner.

INTERVIEWER: Did you [Debby] know how your marriage would be set up before you got married?

DEBBY: No. Maybe you did, but I didn't.

DARYL: I had an inkling, but you never know quite how things are going to work out.

INTERVIEWER: When did you find out, Debby?

DEBBY: After we got married.

INTERVIEWER: How soon?

DEBBY: Very soon. Within the first week.

INTERVIEWER: Why do you think you didn't pick this up before you were married?

DEBBY: I don't know. Probably because we weren't together for that long a time. We'd see each other two or three times a week.

DARYL: Yes.

DEBBY: But it was all on a—you know, he'd cook supper, or we'd go out—on a date basis. Now he comes home for supper every night and I've got to have it on the table.

Perhaps the most significant point made by Debby was that before they were married, they would sometimes get together at Daryl's apartment (Debby lived with her parents), and Daryl would cook supper, but that after they were married, Daryl demanded that she take over the cooking. This is significant because it opens the possibility that the reason that their differing conceptions of marital roles were not realized was *not* that they were rarely in a position where their differences might come to a head, as Debby claimed, but that Daryl did not begin to act chauvinistically until Debby became his wife. Only then was she the incumbent of the wife position. Additional support for this contention is provided when Daryl admits that he "had an inkling" that the marriage would be set up the way it was. Perhaps he anticipated the role transition. This is not the only possible explanation. There is also the possibility that Daryl did tell Debby beforehand what he would be demanding of her as his wife but that Debby did not listen (selective inattention, perhaps) or that she planned to change Daryl, that once she and he were married, she would "manipulate" him to her way of thinking: ("I've watched my mother manipulate my father for years.")

Debby's original plan was to find a job soon after she got married. She evidently believed, even during the first months of marriage and while she was looking for work, that Daryl's demands on her to be the chief cook and bottle washer would be altered. As she saw it, he could not possibly want her to be a full-time housewife if she were working full time. The first problem she encountered in trying to implement her plan was not being able to find a job. Marrying Daryl meant, at least in the beginning, living close to where Daryl worked. The company with which Daryl was associated, however, was located in a remote area of New England. Teaching or even secretarial positions--the types of jobs for which she was willing to work--were scarce. She did get one break. One of the secretaries who worked for Daryl's firm quit and Debby was offered her job. Much to her surprise, though she was still working full time, Daryl still expected her to "take care of him." What resulted was, in Debby's words, "a big battle royal."

DARYL: It's tough taking care of me. She couldn't work full time and take care of me. That couldn't be possible.

INTERVIEWER: What makes you say that?

DARYL: I just demand a lot of care, that's all.

DEBBY: He says that because—

DARYL: I say that because I don't like to do dishes, vacuuming—
I don't really care about doing those things—and if she worked,
then we'd have to share in those duties. So I would rather that
she did them and not have to work and I'll supply, as well as can
be [expected], the money to run the household.

DEBBY: I worked with him two weeks last spring as a secretary because their girl quit, and I found that after working a ten hour
day bent over a typewriter I was in no mood when I got home
to get his supper or do anything else and it resulted in a big
battle royal.

DARYL: I think we agree that you shouldn't work full time.

DEBBY: That's right.

Note that in the above sequence Debby concurs with
Daryl's assessment that now they both agree that Debby
should not work full time. The implication is that Debby has
conceded to Daryl's definition of the marriage. Daryl had
won the first battle. The war however was not yet over.

Their second major conflict of wills started about the sixth
month of their marriage and was still in progress by the fourth
interview at the end of the pregnancy. They had been renting
since they were married and were in the market for a house.
The question was where to live. Daryl wanted to stay pretty
much where they were. It was close to his work, his parents,
his friends. What is more, in this area he was more likely to
find a house with enough land to accommodate his ham radio
antennas. Living in an apartment had prevented Daryl from
moving his rig from his parent's back yard. Debby wanted to
move closer to where her parents and friends lived. She did
not like living at "the end of the world." Moving closer to a
city meant that she could be near all her favorite shopping
places. Perhaps most important, she might be able to find
a job.

DEBBY: This seems like the end of the world up here. It's completely
removed from [small city] and all the places I like to go shop-

ping, and all the people I know. . . . I just find this town kind of suffocating. If I really wanted to go to work, I couldn't because there aren't any jobs around here.

During the fourth interview, I asked the couple who they thought was in charge of their marriage. Their discussion of the issue is interesting because it illustrates the logic Daryl used to support his belief that where to live was his domain while demonstrating the conflicts in Debby's personal conceptions between what *was* and what she believed *should be*. It is also an interesting sequence in that it shows the importance of labels in the intersubjective world.

INTERVIEWER: Do you feel that anyone is in charge in this marriage?

DEBBY: No.

DARYL: Although if you talk in terms of president and vice-president —

DEBBY: He'd be president, right dear?

DARYL: I suppose.

DEBBY: Yes, you're probably in charge.

DARYL: . . . I thought that fit pretty well. Didn't you?

DEBBY: How about president and chairman of the board? I don't think president/vice-president is very good. A vice-president is usually a yes man who goes along with everything the president says. I don't like that. We've gone through that before and found that it doesn't work.

INTERVIEWER: What do you mean you've gone through that before?

DEBBY: We went through that over where we wanted to live. He wanted to buy the house we rented this past summer. He said he was going to buy it. I finally made him see that if he bought it, I wasn't going to live with him. . . . That's why I don't like the idea of president/vice-president. Chairman of the board. For equal voice.[3]

INTERVIEWER: Is that how you see it Daryl?

DARYL: [Begrudgingly] Well, yeah, I suppose so.

INTERVIEWER: Daryl, what did you mean by president/vice-president?

DARYL: I suppose that if we had some big decisions to make, I would probably have to make final a situation.

DEBBY: And I don't agree with that at all. If it can't be a mutual decision, then I don't think it's a decision worth making.

Daryl then shifts his strategy and claims that the reason he should be in charge of the house buying is that he is likely to be the more forceful and strike a better deal. Debby has no qualms with this explanation. Perhaps she sees Daryl's justification as less sexist (Daryl is the more competent bargainer). When he returns to more of an ideological line (he should be president because "that's the way it should be") she tells me he's a chauvinist.

DARYL: The point about deciding on the house—I direct how that will occur . . . because I would probably be more forceful. If somebody said, "It's this much," you'd say, "Oh, OK." And I'd say, "Is that right? We'll go somewhere else."

DEBBY: I see your point.

INTERVIEWER: Debby, you had said that this was a source of conflict.

DARYL: It was a source of conflict—deciding where to live.

DEBBY: It was more general. [Was Daryl trying to generalize his right to make this decision to all major decisions?] You went on and said you'd be the one to make the decision. And I just couldn't agree with you. You make the decision as long as I agree with the decision you're making. . . . Because I can get very nasty. That's why it was a point. I absolutely hated this house. I detested the place. I loathed every second we lived there and he kept talking about buying it.

INTERVIEWER: Daryl, why do you think you should be the president?

DARYL: I just think that's the way it should be, that's all.

DEBBY: He's a male chauvinist.

Debby has no objection to Daryl claiming authority if he bases his claim on competency. Authority claimed in this way is more objective and subject to change. For example, Debby could gain competence in an area and command Daryl's respect. What Debby objects to is Daryl's chauvinism—his ideological claims to power. Authority claimed in this way is more difficult, if not impossible, to change; Debby can not change her sex. These two claims to power—competency and ideology—represent the two theories of power most often discussed by sociologists. Actually, competency is one way power may be gained under the resource theory which states that power in a marriage is based on the comparative resources which the husband and wife bring to the marriage. "A resource may be defined as anything that one partner may make available to the other, helping the latter satisfy his needs or attain his goals" (Blood and Wolfe, 1960: 12). Besides competency, resources may include money, perhaps the most important resource for satisfying needs and attaining goals. Thus, the more powerful spouse is the more competent individual or the primary wage earner. The ideological theory, on the other hand, states that power is based on beliefs and values. What the culture says is the way it is supposed to be. Thus, the more powerful spouse is whoever the culture prescribes. If the culture is patriarchal, the husband will rule.

At this point Debby introduces her theory on why they have differing conceptions on how a marriage should work. She explains, as previously noted, that she believes it all has to do with the way they were raised, that in his house the father was the boss, but that in her home her mother manipulated her father. This prompts Daryl to ask whether she manipulates him.

DARYL: Well, how come you don't do it that way? Or do you do that?

DEBBY: I always get my own way, don't I?

INTERVIEWER: How do you get your own way?

DEBBY: Various methods. I don't want to go into it. Those are trade
    secrets.

Debby leaves little doubt that, if only on an informal,
under the table level, she does in fact exert control on the
marriage. Her point is noteworthy because it raises the distinction between formal and informal control. The formal
control structure is the explicit command hierarchy in a
social organization. The informal control structure is the
implicit network of influence which operates parallel to or,
sometimes, in contradiction to the formal hierarchy. In the
military, for example, though lieutenants are formally higher
than sergeants, quite often it is the sergeant who commands
more respect and has more influence in a unit. How many
traditional patriarchal families are actually run behind the
scenes by the wife-mother?

Daryl then shifts his strategy again. He draws a distinction
between the "inside world" and the "outside world." His
marriage constitutes the inside world. Everything else is the
outside world. Where he is "the president" is at the "interface" between the two worlds, and that decision-making
which is limited in scope to the inside world is, perhaps, on
a "much more equal basis." He claims, and Debby agrees,
that buying a house is part of the interface. but he concedes
that his authority at the interface (taxes, money, terms)
would only be used *"if [they] found a house that [they]
both liked!"*

DARYL: My presidency of the marriage is in terms of the interface
    between the inside world and the outside world.

INTERVIEWER: How about the inside world?

DARYL: That may be much more on an equal basis.

INTERVIEWER: Do you see buying a house on a basis with the
    outside world?

DARYL: Yes.

DEBBY: As far as tax, and discussing money and terms, and stuff
    like that.

DARYL: . . . That's one interface. If we found a house that we both liked, then the interface would be mine—like offering this many dollars less than what they're asking. . . .

DEBBY: I think it started out that he had the idea that I would just go along with whatever he wanted to do about living there. I thought that he thought he was acting as a president in making the decision. I don't think it was so much the house as being told I was going to live there.

The fact that this indicates a serious change in Daryl's previous position is noted by Debby, who claims that Daryl "started out" with the idea that whether or not she liked the house was unimportant. She closes by stating that it was not the house as much as it was being told where she was going to live. Score one for Debby.

Thus far I have outlined two major areas of conflict for Daryl and Debby—*work* (Debby's job and the division of labor within the home) and *decision-making* (specifically, the rules for decision-making in their marriage). Both of these areas fall within what is usually termed the instrumental aspects of the marriage. The third major area of conflict falls within the noninstrumental (sometimes called the expressive or affective) sphere of the marriage. Specifically, it has to do with Daryl and Debby's *recreational activities*. As noted, Daryl worked to play. In fact so involved was he in his play activities, that when I asked him why his marriage worked, he answered in unequivocally utilitarian terms (cf., Cuber and Harroff, 1965).

INTERVIEWER: Why do you think your marriage works?

DARYL: I think it works because, first off, probably the necessities that one needs to accomplish are fulfilled by each of us. The problem is easier, or less painful, than if we tried to do all the things necessary for one person to do. And I would say that it's easier for me to go to work, and it's easier for Debby to do the food and washing and so forth than it would be for either of us to do both. That's definitely a fit right there. It's quite important. I think also that we don't do all of what we do together, but I think what we do, watching television, playing cards, and maybe go visit somebody, whatever, or go shopping, we enjoy, or at least I do. And . . . I'm given enough free time to do what I may want to do, like work on the ham radio, or the car, or go fishing, or something like that. And I think she's given the same opportunity. I think free time is very important, whether you're married or not.

The conflict within the recreational sphere centered principally on Daryl's involvement with recreational activities which excluded Debby. The activity which annoyed Debby the most and which she saw as a waste of time was the activity Daryl enjoyed the most—ham radio competition.

DEBBY: I see ham radio competition as a waste of time.

INTERVIEWER: Why do you think Debby thinks it's a waste of time?

DARYL: . . . Because it's time that's spent away from her.

DEBBY: You're probably right.

The weekend competitions required that Daryl go to his parents' home, where his radio was set up. Typically, he would be gone for just about the whole two days. Daryl's exclusion of Debby in his play activities was actually congruent with his chauvinistic ideology. Daryl advocated conjugal role segregation (see Bott, 1971: 53) not only with respect to work roles and decision-making but also in recreation. Debby, on each of these fronts, was more in favor of a joint conjugal role relationship (see Bott, 1971: 53). She wanted to share in the economic functions of the marriage. She wanted Daryl to share more in the division of household tasks. She advocated a more democratic form of decision-making or, at the very least, a criterion for decision making, namely resources, which permitted authority to be more objective and capable of change. Finally, she wanted Daryl and her to spend more of their free time doing things together rather than apart.

Given the gap between what Debby *wanted* in her marriage and what she *had,* having a baby was, in fact, the "logical thing to do!" Through parenthood she could gain a lever on Daryl. She could use her pregnancy and the baby to restructure her marriage to her conceptions. Whereas the early months of their marriage required a change in plans for Debby, parenthood would force Daryl to change his ways in a direction which would bring him more into line with Debby's ideas on what he should be doing. The irony of the situation is that Debby did not, in my opinion, consciously decide to get pregnant as a power move. Having a baby, first of all, was "logical" because Daryl did not really give her much choice. During the first interview, when I asked how they came to the decision to have a baby, Daryl said the decision was really Debby's (another example of conjugal role segregation), that she was not sure what she would be doing, and that she had to choose between working or having a child (he considered the two mutually exclusive). As we have already seen, Daryl foreclosed on one of Debby's options (working), so in effect she had no real choice. Couple the fact that she was forced to stay home with the peer pressure from her friends ("so many of our friends have adorable babies"), and it becomes quite understandable how parenthood seemed so "logical." It gave her something worthwhile to do—other than cooking and cleaning. It legitimated her role as a housewife. After Debby got pregnant, I believe she began to see that having a child was also "logical" in another sense. Whereas the woman who leaves her job because she is a mother may lose power in her marriage (the amount of money/resources she brings to the marriage declines), the woman who is a housewife when she gets pregnant may begin to gain power in her marriage. First, it is typically the wife who is deemed the one to know about childcare. Therefore, motherhood increases the wife's relative competency. Second, pregnancy and motherhood give the wife legitimate reasons for withholding satisfaction and goal attainment (resources) from her husband (e.g., I'm too ill . . . I'm taking care of the baby now.). Third, the wife may use the child to gain benefits for herself. She may demand that her husband spend more time at home with the child (Be a father!) and thus covertly force him to spend more time at home with her (Be a husband!).

Debby began to make her first moves during the pregnancy itself. Like many husbands of pregnant wives, Daryl expected that, given his wife's condition, he would be doing more of the duties around the house. What he evidently did not anticipate was Debby's attempts to normalize his helping her. By normalize I mean redefining an activity from atypical (and therefore worthy of recognition) to typical. Although I was able to pick up only one instance of this negotiation process, its existence does raise the possibility that there were other tasks which were being traded. The task in question is a simple one—carrying the laundry bag from the house up the hill to the car so Debby could wash the clothes at the laundromat. What made the task difficult for Debby was the fact that there was a hill. Before she was pregnant, Debby carried the clothes to the car. Thus, for her to request that Daryl do it was atypical and worthy of recognition (Thank you for doing something which you normally don't have to do.). As the pregnancy progressed, and as Debby got larger, it seems that Debby began to take it for granted that Daryl would carry the laundry up the hill, thereby normalizing the activity. Daryl sensed (and resented?) this and asked "Why?" Debby claimed that it provided an excuse to put off doing the laundry (something she couldn't get away with before, evidently). Perhaps, what she meant by this is that she could now argue that it was Daryl's fault if the laundry did not get done (You weren't here to carry the laundry to the car.).

INTERVIEWER: Have you noticed any changes since I last spoke with you?

DARYL: I noticed that I've been carrying the laundry up sometimes. You wouldn't attempt some things that you may have attempted previously.

DEBBY: Yes. That's true.

DARYL: There's got to be some reason for that. Why was that?

DEBBY: It's just too heavy.

DARYL: Oh. I see.

DEBBY: It gets very awkward trying to carry that laundry basket when you're carrying it out far. You don't have quite the sense of balance that you do when it's close to you.

DARYL: Yes, but you *could* do it.

DEBBY: Yea, I could do it.

DARYL: Well, why didn't you do it?

DEBBY: Why not let *you* do it?

DARYL: I don't know. I'm just trying to figure out why you didn't do it.

DEBBY: I just didn't feel like it. Besides, it was an excuse not to go to the laundromat anymore.

INTERVIEWER: So you've been doing the laundry more, Daryl?

DARYL: No, I haven't been doing it, but coming up this hill several months previously, she would carry it up the hill. Now there's no question that I carry it up the hill.

INTERVIEWER: When did you start carrying it up the hill?

DARYL: A couple of months ago. But it seemed to be a more intense feeling, that there was no question that you would not carry it up the hill. It just wouldn't get done.

DEBBY: I told you it was an excuse!

INTERVIEWER: Does that mean that you expect this to continue after the baby's born, Daryl?

DARYL: Oh, no!

During the second interview, Debby explicitly mentioned that she felt the pregnancy gave her the feeling that she could say anything she felt like saying and that nobody dare do anything about it because they had no "weight" (no pun intended by me or Debby). Hearing this, Daryl replied that he had not noticed that. Debby's comeback implies that she is using the art of spousal manipulation learned from her mother. While Daryl's power may be more obvious, Debby's guerilla approach is not necessarily any less potent.

DEBBY: I just have a feeling that I can say anything I feel like saying and nobody dares do anything about it! Isn't that awful?

INTERVIEWER: Do you think that's related to the pregnancy?

DEBBY: Yes. Who is going to say anything to me now? They have no weight.

DARYL: I never noticed that.

DEBBY: Just keep on *not* noticing it, and we'll get along fine.

As I mentioned, when Daryl made the comment that the decision to have the baby was in Debby's hands, he gave the impression that as far as he was concerned, parenthood was Debby's domain. By the fourth interview, after attending the childbirth classes (which from my conversations with the couples had the very definite effect of convincing husbands to go into the delivery room with their wives), Daryl began to feel that, like it or not, he was very much a part of the whole affair.

DARYL: It looks like *we* are going to the hospital and *we* are going to have a baby by the looks of these classes.

DEBBY: Your attitude has changed considerably since you went to the classes.

Debby evidently intended to make sure that Daryl continued in this vein after the baby was born. She could understand if Daryl did not want to help with the diapering or if he wanted to spend time with his child when he (the baby) was in a good mood. She just wanted to see Daryl spend time with the baby—perhaps more time than Daryl, himself, intended to spend. Debby's demand can be interpreted in two ways. First, it is an attempt to incorporate Daryl into the parental role. Second, it may have been an attempt to manipulate Daryl into spending more time with Debby. One may wonder how many family outings would be planned for weekends on which ham radio competitions were also scheduled. Finally, although working did not give her an out from having to take care of Daryl (when she got the full time job, Daryl still expected her to be a full-time maid), the child would give her an excuse to deny Daryl some attention.

DEBBY: I can see where with a third person in the house there will be a change. Obviously, he'll not get my undivided attention as he gets it now.

DARYL: Groan!

DEBBY: [Imitating Daryl] Groan! Hadn't thought about that, had you?

One point needs to be made. At no time did Debby explicitly state that she intended to use motherhood as a lever to bend Daryl to her will. But then again, if Debby did make explicit references to her tactics, she would, in effect, be undermining her whole strategy ("Just keep on *not* noticing it, and we'll get along fine.").

NOTES

1. The definition of crisis I am using is the one used by W.I. Thomas. Thomas's theory of crisis is discussed in Volkart's (1951) introduction.

2. In ham radio competitions, one's score is determined by how many other operators one can contact in a given time period and how far (geographically) these contacts are.

3. Debby implies that she would be chairman of the board and Daryl would be president—"for equal voice." But chairman of the board is formally higher than president!

Chapter 3

HANK AND HELEN

For Hank and Helen, pregnancy signaled essentially one thing—the end of the conflict over "when to have a child, when to become a family?" They had always assumed that at some time in their married life, they would become parents. As Hank said during one of the interviews, they never seriously considered not having children (at least not "out loud"). The question was, "When?" The pattern that developed was Helen wanting a child "now" and Hank opting for "later." The disagreement reached serious proportions at the end of their second year of marriage when they considered a separation to try to "work things out." After one meeting with a counselor, they decided to stay together.

Hank did most of the talking during the interviews. I often found it difficult to get Helen to express her opinions. Consequently, throughout this chapter I have had to rely, to a large extent, on Hank's quotes as data for Helen's thoughts and feelings. Much of our discussion during the sessions revolved around Hank's reconstructing for me the past four years of their marriage. He especially wanted me to appreciate what the pregnancy meant to him, how far they had come. In fact, whenever they spoke about the pregnancy (how they felt about it, what had happened since my last visit with them) or projected themselves into the postnatal period (how they would feel, what they would be doing), they were always positive. Not once did they ever have anything negative to say. Hank and Helen were the only couple in the sample (of the sixteen) to do this. Some couples, of course, were more positive than others. But, with the exception of Hank and Helen, no couple was completely positive about their transition to parenthood. They could all find at least one thing that was bad about the pregnancy. They could all entertain the possibility that having children around might prove to be less than wonderful at times. All except Hank and Helen. But then none of the other couples' marriages was saved from divorce by the pregnancy; Hank and Helen's marriage was.

Hank and Helen had known each other for three years before they were married. During that time Hank was in the service, and Helen was enrolled in school studying to become a nurse. Hank was anxious to leave the service and "settle down and get married." Helen wanted to go on for her bachelor's degree in nursing, after which she wanted to gain experience in her field. She "wasn't interested in settling down at that point." She did change her mind, however. What prompted her was Hank's having to take a tour of duty in Europe. It was while they were separated that she "realized she wanted to marry him."

After they married, they reversed roles, so to speak. Hank, who by then had left the service, wanted to go to college and get not only his bachelor's degree but his doctorate. He planned to be a college professor. Helen, on the other hand, was eager to "settle down and start a family." Finances precluded both from having what they wanted. They decided that they would put off having the family for a while; Helen would work full time as a nurse (she scrapped her idea to continue school after she received her nursing license), and Hank would try to get through school as quickly as he could while he brought in money through part-time work and the G.I. bill. Helen was only able to get the evening shift (4 PM—midnight) when she applied at the local hospital. Hank's schedule of classes and work was such that he was home only during the evenings. They rarely saw each other. Even the weekends were taken up. Helen's hospital required that all nurses work every other weekend. Helen described what their situation was like.

HELEN: We were both caught up in our little worlds; he at school and I with my job and it just seemed like we didn't have much of a marriage. We just kind of passed each other now and then.

According to the couple, not being with each other meant that they rarely had the opportunity to "really talk." When they were able to find time to get together, they usually had to catch up on issues that were pressing (e.g., bills). Very infrequently did they just visit with each other. Not being able to engage in an exchange of ideas during the early phases of their marriage may have contributed to the fact that Hank and Helen lived in two "little worlds" in more ways than one.

With respect to their discussions to put off starting a family, Hank said that before they got married, they had sat down and discussed the whole thing and pretty much settled how they would work it (and why they were doing what they were doing) beforehand. The first time they began to suspect that their arrangement to wait was not as settled as they thought was during the first year of their marriage when Hank happened to ask Helen what she thought of living in Washington, D.C., explaining that, given his specialty (one of the social sciences), they could very well end up there. Helen was stunned. She had been born and raised in New England and had always planned to raise her family there too. She had no idea that Hank was considering leaving. She began to question the value of his education if it meant leaving the area she loved, and the area she thought Hank loved too. Hank, whose family was with the military when he was a child (his self-description: "someone without roots"), did love New England, but he was unwilling to jeopardize his career just to stay there.

HANK: She wanted to stay close to New England, and I kind of like New England too. I didn't want to feel that if there wasn't something in New England that I wanted to do, I'd be trapped into staying, and working at a job. She's a New England girl. She's been out of the area maybe three times in her life. Before I married her, once in her life. I should have sensed it. And one day in the conversation it came out. "How about if I ended up with a job in Washington?" It was then that I realized that we didn't see eye to eye on this. At the time, things were pressing, and things were hard, and we didn't know each other that well. In light of some of the arguments we have had, that didn't get blown all out of proportion because we did manage to talk about it.

What disturbed Helen, however, was not that Hank would be unwilling to stay in New England if he had to choose between it or his career. What disturbed her was what she felt this signified that—contrary to what she thought Hank believed in—Hank was self-centered rather than family-centered. She felt that he was putting his own interests above the family's. Actually, Hank's concern for his career, and for himself, were, according to Hank's definition of marriage and the family, not selfish but ultimately for the family. The fact is Hank and Helen each had different conceptions of what the institution of marriage was all about—what it should be.

Helen's definition of marriage was that it was a relationship in which two people became one; it was the giving of oneself to one's spouse.

HELEN: Marriage is just two people becoming very close together. I don't know. You want to do things *for* the other person, you want to do things *with* the other person. In marriage you love the other person and you become one. You want to do everything for him.

The rules of such a marriage, according to Helen, specified a relationship of togetherness. Individual pursuits (e.g., working) were permitted, but only because they were necessary to support the family. Too much individuality was a symptom and a major cause of marital failure. Hank's schooling was permissable provided it was defined as a means to an end—the family.

Hank's definition of marriage was that of a relationship in which two people become one but without losing their selves.

HANK: Marriage is a commitment to a common identity which compels sacrifice. It is a surrendering of your own identity to a common identity. . . . It entails a sense of selflessness, of surrendering the self to a common identity. . . . It's possible [however] to go too far into it, to wake up one morning and to find that you've lost yourself . . . and that frame of mind is broken.

The rules of such a marriage, according to Hank, specified a relationship in which autonomy was not simply tolerated—it was desirable. A husband or wife should seek things to do which don't include the other. Too much togetherness was a symptom and a major cause of marital failure.

HANK: I think that an awful lot of people that divorce . . . do it because they had realized that the selflessness had perhaps gone too far.

For Hank, his schooling was a means to an end; it was ultimately for the family. But it was for the family in a way different from what Helen's system dictated. Yes, the family would benefit from the fact that he would be able to translate his schooling into monetary gains. But more important than this gain was his belief that by personally developing himself, he would be contributing to the family's development. By not "losing himself" in the marriage, the marriage would be maintained.[1]

The fact that Hank and Helen had differing conceptions of the husband-wife relationship introduces another reason why when they were able to find time in their hectic schedules to be together, they didn't "really talk." Hank spoke of the problem they had when they had an evening at home.

HANK: Like when I come home I like to settle back a little and relax. I like to be able to sit down and spend an hour reading the *Times* in the evening and then spend a couple of hours reading a book, or instead of reading work on my painting. She wants, "Let's do something together." And for me, she's sitting here reading or knitting, and I'm sitting at the desk painting and we chat back and forth about things that happened during the day, *are* doing things. But not for her. Doing things together, for her, means me here and she about there [both on the couch, about a foot apart] and that's how we get our conversation and everything else. And I just don't feel like doing that. "Come on, do something else. I want to do my thing for a while. Move over and give me a little bit of room!" . . . we compromise and everything works out all right.

Returning to the New England controversy, Hank mentioned that "in light of some of the arguments" they had had over the course of their marriage, this argument "didn't get blown all out of proportion" because they managed to "talk about it." Whatever they said, they did not change the way they lived. That is, Hank continued to go to school and Helen continued to work. What they implied *did* change was the way they thought about what they were doing. Helen began to believe they were just wasting their time as long as they continued without starting a family.

HANK: I saw her at times waiting, every day was just another day wasted without a family being started. And she couldn't stand the waiting, wanting to stay home and be a mother.

Hank started to wonder whether he was doing "the right thing."

HANK: I was in a real rut and depressed about one thing or another and caught up in school and I wasn't sure I was doing the right thing.

At the end of their second year of marriage, Helen encountered some problems with her menstruation cycle. Despite the fact they were trying not to have a baby, they were faced with the possibility that she might be pregnant. The different reactions each had toward the possibility prompted an argument which did get "blown all out of proportion." It turned out that Helen was not pregnant. However, as a consequence of what they had said to each other during the crisis, they concluded that it might be best if they saw a professional. They were seriously thinking about separating.

During the fourth and final interview, Hank and Helen confessed that they had once considered separating. Previously, when I asked them about the early years of their marriage they would never be very specific. They always left me with the impression that something was being left unsaid. Finally, in the last interview I asked them outright, "Was there ever any time in your marriage that you considered getting a divorce?" There was a long pause. Then Hank started to speak, "No. Not divorce. But. . . . " I asked what kind of professional they had seen.

HANK: She wasn't in the marriage counselor business. She was a counselor. She had a doctorate in clinical psychology.

Each of them had met privately with the counselor. I asked them to describe what happened during their respective sessions.

HELEN: I don't think she told me anything much. I did most of the talking. She just said back to me what I had said and kind of made me listen to what I was saying. And I don't remember any real advice that she gave other than to stay open and communicate with each other.

HANK: It was just a matter of going in and she'd say, "What's on your mind? What do you imagine to be the problem?" And we'd talk to her and she'd say, "Well, what about this attitude or that attitude?"

You will note that when Hank speaks of what transpired during the session, he says that the psychologist focused on what was on his mind, and then she asked, "Well, what about this attitude or that attitude?" Helen's session preceded Hank's. The attitudes the psychologist was asking Hank to think about were Helen's attitudes; Helen's conceptions and definitions. Hank was being introduced (for the first time?) to his wife! They never followed through on their separation.

By asking Hank and Helen what happened during their respective sessions with the psychologist, I prompted a discussion which gave me a detailed picture of the couple's conceptions and interactional patterns, not only during the first two years of their marriage but during the last two years as well. The reasons for this were, first of all, that the couple did not remain on a descriptive level but retrospectively evaluated the sessions; and, second, many of the problems which the psychologist raised were not remedied by the sessions. In some respects, the sessions merely made the couple aware of their problems. Working out these problems was a perennial task for Hank and Helen.

HANK: We had been married two years and still—How do you marry? How do you act married? What's the proper way of being married? Rather than just you're married, we were still working this out.

HELEN: . . . We were just not communicating and I think that is where we just kind of fell down instead of talking things out. . . .

HANK: I think on my part. . . . I'd tell her it's senseless to feel that way. I was giving her feelings that she didn't feel. I was assuming things on her part and then responding to my assumptions rather than to what she really was. She'd feel sorry sometimes about not having a family and I'd tell her, "You don't have to feel sorry about that. We've talked about it before, about holding off on it. You don't need to feel sorry." And it was wrong, I know now, to tell her because those were honest legitimate feelings and they had to be dealt with. It couldn't be swept under the rug as having no basis because for her they had a real basis. What the woman [the psychologist] did for me was just plain and simple. She'd listen and she said it back and I couldn't believe what I was saying when she said it back to me. I had taken a very protective, overbearing role toward Helen and I thought I had kept a very understanding open approach. But in reality I was very closed and had a very narrow mind about what she should be doing, and what she shouldn't be doing.

In the above sequence, Hank makes two essential points about how he was acting toward Helen. First, he says that he would act toward Helen on the basis of what he assumed she was like rather than what she "really" was like. We all act on the basis of our assumptions. What Hank seems to be saying, however, is that he was ignoring Helen, not validating her feelings. The term used to denote this problem is disconfirmation. More devastating than rejection, which tells the listener that he is wrong, disconfirmation says, in effect, that he does not exist (Watzlawick et al., 1967: 86). Secondly, Hank says that he had taken a very protective, overbearing role toward Helen. It would seem, given his comments, that Hank was placing the blame for the state of their marriage on himself. Actually, this is only half the picture. From what the couple said and from what I observed, there is evidence to suggest that, at times, Helen contributed to her own disconfirmation and subordination through her introversion and dependency. The fact is that Hank and Helen were involved in a vicious interactional cycle. By a vicious interactional cycle I mean what Watzlawick et al. (1967: 46, 58) meant when they spoke of the circularity of communication patterns. The illustration they used is the husband-wife cycle—nag-withdraw-nag-withdraw—in which one partner's nagging causes the other's withdrawal, which causes the former's nagging, and so on. The point is that it is meaningless to speak of a beginning because the series is a feedback system. The parties involved may see what they believe to be the cause of the cycle (e.g., I nag him because he withdraws) but this is an example of what Watzlawick et al. (1967: 54) call punctuating the sequence. Punctuation is simply the cognitive organization of behavior.

The introversion-disconfirmation cycle was illustrated during the interviews. As noted previously, Hank provided most of the answers to my questions. Helen spoke very little. Often her silence prompted Hank to speak for her. That is, if I asked the couple how they felt individually about something, Helen would frequently defer to Hank and Hank would then tell me how he felt and how he thought Helen felt. On these occasions, when I would then turn to Helen to try to get her to tell me in her own words how she felt, she would say, "Hank said it all." The impression I received from sequences such as this is that Helen's introversion was the cause of Hank's not knowing how Helen "really" felt and his having to rely on his "assumptions." There were occasions, however, when the causal order seemed to be reversed. Sometimes I would direct a question specifically at Helen (that is, I would say her name and look straight at her). She would try to answer, but Hank would intercede and answer for her. It was as if she was not in the room! Whether or not Hank realized what he was doing (that he was not permitting Helen to tell me—and him—how she "really" felt) is an open question. One comment made during the third interview pointed to the possibility that he was not aware that he in effect was disconfirming her. The comment was made in connection with their telling me what they talked about after I left them. Hank said that after the second interview, Helen told him that he had "talked a lot," that he had gotten "carried away." Hank remarked that he "never saw it that way," that he would admit "there were times" when he might "go off with something," but this was "very rare, very rare." The transcripts give evidence to the contrary. In fact, Hank's remark came at the end of a sequence in which he had just spoken for Helen and she wanted to speak for herself! When I asked the couple whether the interaction pattern which was revealed during the interviews was typical of their everyday pattern, Hank answered, "Yes," and then he told me how this pattern was a problem for him because he was then forced to "piece together things" (guess? create?) in order to find out what was on Helen's mind.

HANK: I see her sitting there quietly which she does very well because that's all she's done by and large for a long time. You know, she's kind of introverted in that fashion. . . . And then there are times when she says, "Well, let's go to bed and talk or let's talk a little." "Well, fine, what are we going to talk about?" And I'm the one who ends up talking and I had nothing to talk about in the first place. Because she says, "Well, things in general." "Well, what about? You got a problem? What's bothering you?" "Well, everything kinda." And I have to interpret that! I have to piece together these things. She doesn't say what's on her mind.

Although Hank's anecdote is supposed to serve as his example of how Helen is the cause of his not being able to "really" know her, the same episode could be used to explain the reverse. That is, if Helen told me her opinion of what happened, would she have punctuated the interaction by saying, "I wanted to talk, but he wouldn't let me get a word in edgewise"? It is my belief that Hank and Helen's introversion-disconfirmation relationship is a circular feedback system.

With respect to the dependency-subordination cycle, the seeds for this interaction cycle were sown before Hank and Helen were married. In fact, "taking care" of Helen was the reason Hank gave when he decided to marry her. What is noteworthy in the following passage is Hank's attributing his accomplishments to Helen. It was her confidence in him (dependence on him?) that gave him strength. Strength to do what? Take care of Helen.

INTERVIEWER: What was it about Helen that made you decide to marry her?

HANK: She just radiated confidence. And when I was with her, she'd give me every confidence in the world. She provided me with something long before I ever considered marrying her, just something that gave me a little bit of self support. It helped me. What I didn't have in myself for accomplishing things that I wanted to accomplish she provided just by being with me. I thought of doing things in terms of the confidence she gave me. That I think, and the fact that she's such a little girl. I mean she's so small. I just wanted to take care of her. What's strange is that when I met her she was extremely thin as well. I guess I just wanted to take her home and take care of her. I was attracted to her because of what she did for me and then I didn't want to leave her out in the cold after she'd given me all the confidence in the world. I just wanted to take her along because she was so good to me.

How much different is the above description from the one below in which Hank discusses what he realized after speaking with the psychologist. He starts out by coming down hard on himself ("I was making rather major decisions with very little consideration for her"), implying that he is the cause of her dependency. He concludes, however, by implying the reverse ("Because she took advantage of my doing that"). Once again, the pattern is cyclical.

HANK: I realized that I was perhaps being extremely unfair to her. By not letting her do it herself—even minor details, say keeping track of the checkbook—I was making rather major decisions with very little consideration for her. Even sometimes without asking her. Because I felt, perhaps, she couldn't make the decision on her own, wasn't qualified to make the decision. I had disregarded whatever her thoughts were as being unimportant and it was kind of a hard realization. Because she then, I think, kind of took advantage of my doing that and I used to get a little upset that I was babysitting that way.

Of course, the two cycles (introversion-disconfirmation and dependency-subordination) are interrelated. Perhaps the best example of this relationship is a sequence which took place during the third interview. Hank was accusing Helen of being dependent on him.

HANK: She just lets herself become dependent on me. . . .

INTERVIEWER: What do you think, Helen?

HELEN: I think I can be assertive at times.

HANK: Yes, if I prompt her.

The critical statement is Hank's "Yes, if I prompt her." With it he essentially negates Helen's claim that she can be assertive. He does so by describing how he has disconfirmed her independency by accepting only those "times" in which he "prompted" Helen to be assertive. All other "times" (times which Helen may have thought she was being assertive) do not qualify as assertive and therefore do not exist (under the category assertive). The only "times" that do qualify, however, can not be categorized by Helen as assertive because she was prompted. Having been "prompted," she can no longer claim she was the initiator, but must give Hank the credit for motivating her.

If the above exchange is typical, it is understandable why Helen is confused over whether she is dependent or not, as she indicates below.

> HELEN: I let myself become dependent on him. It's my own doing, but then other times I can be very independent. Just sometimes it's hard to tell the difference between the two.

R.D. Laing's comments on the effects of disconfirmation are most appropriate in this regard. The individual's "feelings are denuded of validity, his acts are stripped of their motives, intentions and consequences, the situation is robbed of its meaning for him, so that he is totally mystified and alienated" (Laing, 1961: 135-136). The point—Hank can subordinate Helen by his words as well as by his deeds.

At the end of their third year of marriage, Hank and Helen came to a crossroad in their lives. Hank had managed to get his bachelor's degree in three years. The question before them was "parenthood—now or later?" Hank said that they "sat down and talked to each other" and "straightened each other out." What it seems they did was to construct a compromise. Agreed: they would live in New England because that was the best place to raise a family. Agreed: with only a bachelor's degree, it was doubtful that Hank could get a job that he liked in the New England area; Hank would go on to graduate school for his M.A., after which he would apply for a position—the Ph.D. would have to wait. Agreed: they would try to conceive a child the first semester of graduate school (assuming Hank would finish his master's in one year, parenthood would coincide with Hank's graduation and Helen's resignation from the hospital).

At the time of my first interview with Hank and Helen, they were approximately twelve weeks into the pregnancy. Hank was going to school and looking for a college teaching position for the fall semester. Helen was working the evening shift at the local hospital. When I asked Hank how he felt about the job market, he said he felt "confident." When I asked him whether he felt pressured in his job hunt because of the soon to be added responsibilities of parenthood, he said that on the contrary, the pregnancy "took the edge off the negative replies" from employers, that it served as a "galvanizing factor," and a protection against the pressure. Helen's responses were similarly optimistic. I left the first interview believing that they were being inordinately ideal, perhaps naive. What I came to understand during the succeeding interviews was that parenthood might very well have saved their marriage from divorce. Their pregnancy pointed to a negotiated settlement between them. For the first time in their marriage, Hank and Helen would be able to live in harmony. But—and this is extremely important—the order to their marriage would not be a consequence of their having finally come to a consensual view of their relationship as much as it would be a result of their having created a situation in which they could live with the other's view. The term that has been used to denote this form of arrangement is cooperation. The essence of the cooperative arrangement is that it is not based on attitudinal similarity or value consensus but on a set of shared, mutually understood, procedural rules. The parties to such as arrangement are not concerned with the abolition of existing differences but with their effective management (Sprey, 1969: 703-704). Parenthood would mark a structural change which would facilitate the effective management of Hank and Helen's differences.

By the second interview, Hank had found a job. It was a nonacademic position, but it offered what Hank sas as "potential." It would require that Hank finish his M.A. part-time (his employer wanted him to start immediately), but that also did not bother Hank ("I don't have to rush with my thesis"). It was a New England-based organization. Initially, it seemed that Hank made some real concessions. Actually, he had not conceded that which was most important to him. He had found a job he considered personally fulfilling. His personal growth, as he saw it, would benefit the family. Helen was happy that Hank was doing something he enjoyed. She was also happy to be able to stay in New England. She too was doing something she had wanted to do for a long time—she was becoming a mother. Furthermore, since she would be quitting work at the end of the pregnancy, she and Hank would be spending their evenings together. Her and Hank's togetherness, as she saw it, would benefit the family.

The phrase which Hank and Helen used to describe what was happening to them was "everything fitting/falling into place."

HELEN: Just being able to get settled down, to raise a family, Hank's career, and my own career, just fitting everything together in its place. Rather than concentrating on Hank's schooling having priority over having a family. Getting everything to work together.

HANK: And I think an awful lot of this fantastic adjustment has to do with the fact that I've got a good job. I enjoy what I'm doing and, like she says, everything is falling into place.

It is apparent that when they use the phrase, what they mean is that they are each finally getting what they have each wanted all along. When Helen speaks of her own "career," she is referring to her career as a mother. It is significant that she uses the word to describe both her and Hank's life-work (which is one definition of career given by Webster, 1958: 274). One may infer that she considers their work qualitatively different but equally important. The attitude which Helen has toward motherhood is not the same attitude as she has toward her profession. She is not sure when, if at all, she would care to return to nursing. In contrast, when Hank speaks of the "fantastic adjustment" he is making to Helen he implies that the adjustment is more a function of his job than impending fatherhood. Their conflicts still remain; they still differ on what marriage is all about. But their marriage is perhaps more stable than it has ever been.

The most dramatic change to take place during the pregnancy occurred when Helen quit work at the end and became a full-time housewife. Concurrent with her quitting, Hank and Helen moved into a more spacious apartment in order to be nearer to where Hank worked. The couple's fourth and final interview was conducted in their new home.

They loved their new surroundings. They saw the change as symbolic of the change in their lives, and they could not be happier. Everything was "fantastic." They were looking forward to the birth. Now that Helen was not working anymore, they had their evenings to spend together. They considered this one of the best things to happen to them.

HANK: Really, I have a companion now that I didn't have in the past. . . . It gives us an opportunity to just be together. In the past we did not have that much time to talk with each other, so what talking we did usually was about things that were pressing or important. Now we have a chance to do that. We have a little more of a chance to have a little more feedback back and forth.

The fact that they now had the opportunity to give each other "feedback" was encouraging. Perhaps they would finally get to know each other. Indications were that they were heading in this direction. Note both the content and the form of the following sequence. This is one of the few times that Hank defers to Helen and that Helen speaks at length (at least for her) about what *she* thinks.

HANK: She's become, I don't know, what would you call it?

HELEN: More sensitive to your feelings.

HANK: And I think I'm becoming much more sensitive to her.

HELEN: I think the whole thing about the change in our life style is that I'm just more relaxed about it all and I can tune myself into Hank's feelings and if he's tired I'll go to bed early and if he's not I'll stay up [togetherness!] . . . . And I think I'll appreciate him more.

What they would conclude once they knew each other is, at this point, unknown. When I left them, what they were discovering in each other they evidently liked.

HANK: She has a way with plants! . . . Helen didn't talk to plants. Helen was busy. She's got this—but you know, she talks to plants! I can't explain the feeling that comes over me when she does something like that. Wow! I didn't know you talked to plants! I thought you'd be one of those that thought it was strange to talk to plants!

Postscript

Of all the case studies, this is perhaps the most elusive. It was, without a doubt, the hardest to write. In effect, what Hank and Helen did to each other, they did also to me. They never really introduced themselves. While Helen hid behind silence, Hank hid among his abstractions and verbosity. What is interesting is that I left each session with the couple feeling that they had (relative to many of the other couples in the sample) really opened up to me. In fact, Hank and Helen were the first couple I chose to do a case study on because I thought I had so much. I was duped. For no other couple was I forced to infer so much.

NOTE

1. Hank's conception of marriage is somewhat related to what O'Neill and O'Neill (1972) call "open marriage." By the same token, Helen's conception could be categorized as "closed."

Chapter 4

JOE AND JENNIFER

The first pregnancy meant essentially two things to Joe and Jennifer. It meant that after having waited close to four years, they were finally starting a family, something they had always wanted to do. It also signaled a change in their work structure. For the first time since they were married Joe would be the sole wage earner. The significance of this latter point is that Joe intended to use his new position to make a claim for dominance in the marriage.

Joe was a metaphorical speaker. In order to "clarify" a point, he would often relate the issue to the national or international state of affairs. I must confess there were times when I wished he would have been more specific in his answers. I learned however to accept, as others had, that Joe was just "deep."

JENNIFER: Joe is a very deep thinker, and he always has something on his mind. He can drive you right up a wall!

Though Joe did most of the talking, Jennifer was not at a loss for words. Sometimes she found it difficult to get in a word or remember what question I had asked after Joe had picked it up and run with it for a while, but then so did I. When Jennifer did speak, she said what was on her mind—as did Joe; but, as she once said, what it took Joe to say in a paragraph, she said in a sentence. On a number of occasions during the interviews, while Joe was building an argument (and this was particularly true if Joe's argument was an attempt to justify why he should be in charge), a few well placed words by Jennifer, and Joe's edifice would come tumbling down.

Joe and Jennifer knew each other since high school. Their first reaction to each other was, as Jennifer put it, "mutual disgust." Both attributed this to the fact that they were honest types—if they did not like you, they would tell you— and, in the beginning, they told each other more of what they did not like than of what they liked. In time, their hatred turned to love. What attracted them to each other was their similarities—their openness, their aggressiveness, and, interestingly, what they saw as the inability of either to dominate the other. It was a relationship built explicitly on conflict and honesty. (Joe once described Jennifer as his "confessor," and he hers.)

The couple could not recall any specific point at which they decided to get married. "Someplace along the line," it was just assumed. Though they may not have gone through the marriage proposal ritual, the transition to the married state was one they took very seriously. They were a religious couple. Joe, in particular, prided himself on his interpretations of the Bible. They did not believe in divorce. They felt it reflected weakness—a couple's inability to face life's problems.

When they got married, they lived solely on Jennifer's income. Having graduated from high school with a business diploma, she worked as a bookkeeper. Joe was just beginning his third year of college. He was studying to be an accountant.

Actually, for the first three and a half years of their marriage, Jennifer would be the primary wage earner. This was because after Joe was awarded his bachelor's degree, he went on to attend postgraduate business school, which took him a year and a half to complete.

Both believed that the way each of them was raised explained their personalities and why they complemented each other. Jennifer described her premarriage family life as one in which she was the primary decision-maker.

JENNIFER: I was always very independent before I got married. As a matter of fact, my parents were never my rule. I was the rule of my parents.

Joe, on the other hand, was brought up in a patriarchal home—all decisions were made by his father.

JOE: And at my house it was just the opposite. My father was a very strong father image, traditional. "Come to him, your father will decide for you." . . . he wouldn't give me any responsibility.

Jennifer's independence, they felt, was a function of her having been forced to be independent all along. Joe's was a manifestation of his rebellion against his father's autocratic style ("I had to sort of assert myself."). According to Joe, Jennifer came to the marriage wanting to "get rid of" some of her power, and he came "wanting more," so their relationship "worked out all right." Neither would try to dominate the other.

Although Joe claimed that, as his wife, Jennifer would not attempt to rule him, this evidently was not the case. Soon after they were married (during the first two years), they got into a violent struggle for control. Jennifer made a play for power and Joe responded with force. The disclosure of the violent incident was prompted by my asking Jennifer whether she ran things now—that is, did she believe she was "the rule" of Joe as she was "the rule" of her parents and sisters.

INTERVIEWER: Do you think you run things now?

JENNIFER: No. I tried hard, though!

JOE: She tries. One day we had a conflict and she more or less tried to run me and I told her no, and she got hysterical and said, "I could kill you!" And I got rather angry and slapped her in the face three or four times and I said "Don't you ever say that to me again!" And we haven't had any problems since. So she's sort of learned that she isn't going to dominate.

JENNIFER: Yes, and I kind of like the idea, too.

JOE: She threw a temper tantrum when she realized that she couldn't dominate me, and when she started getting hysterical . . . that's the last time, kid! Yeah, that's the worst argument we ever had! That was a drawn out bang out fight. It lasted about four hours. It sort of built and built. . . .

INTERVIEWER: Were you surprised when Joe hit you?

JOE: Oh, boy, was she.

JENNIFER: Yea.

JOE: She started crying not because I hurt her but because she was shocked—"How dare you!"

INTERVIEWER: Why did you hit her?

JENNIFER: That was a long time ago.

JOE: That was a real long time ago. It's just like if you want to do something like tear down a house, what do you use? Do you use an atom bomb, or do you use a crane and hammers and stuff like that? It's just like physical force. You don't use it until you're forced to use it. At that point, I felt I had to do something physical to stop the bad progression of events. I took my chances with that and it worked. In those circumstances, my judgement was correct and it worked.

JENNIFER: Joe doesn't usually use force. That was the first time and the last time he'll ever do that. It was my fault. I was trying to dominate him, that's for sure. But I was always that type of person, that's why. I always had to be that type of person, because I always had to make my own decisions. I never had anybody else make my decision.

JOE: I'm a very dominating person, too, so there was a conflict there.

JENNIFER: I think that's one of the reasons we get along well, because he was the first person I went out with that I couldn't
dominate. So he was a challenge.

JOE: That was a severe conflict. I don't know if we hadn't solved that
problem, if we would still be married, because of the tension.
I'm not the kind of person that's going to be dominated.

JENNIFER: And I'm not either.

JOE: So we've had to agree, through a process of compromise, and
talking this out. We're living on reconciliation and compromise
and understanding.

INTERVIEWER: Is this an issue that will continue to come up?

JOE: No.

JENNIFER: Because we're closer. No one dominates the other anymore.

JOE: It's not important.

This sequence is important not only for what is said, but
for how as well. First, the tenor of Joe's comments—he
speaks as if Jennifer were guilty of disrespect or even insubor-
dination ("Don't you ever say that to me again!" . . . "That's
the last time, kid!"). Even more, there is undoubtedly a certain amount of pride expressed—he knew he had won the
argument. Jennifer, on the other hand, is quick to point out
"that was the first and the last time he'll ever do that [hit
her]." She wants to make it perfectly clear to me, but more
importantly to Joe, that she too has no intention of being
dominated—and, perhaps, that she considers Joe's gloating
an attempt to do just that! She goes on to admit that she
married Joe because "he was a challenge." Does she mean by
this that she considers Joe her opponent? Finally, though Joe
says at the end that who dominates whom is no longer important, the words he uses to describe their relationship
("We're living on reconciliation and compromise and understanding.") imply that whatever balance they have achieved
(neither dominating the other) it is a negotiated balance.

As noted, Joe was a student for the first three and a half
years of their marriage. When he graduated, he accepted an

offer to work as an accountant with a local firm. One month
after Joe took the job, the couple started trying to conceive a
child. Four months later they found out that Jennifer was
pregnant. They were evidently just biding their time, waiting
for Joe to finish school—the point at which they felt it would
be time to start a family. They always intended to have
children. As Jennifer put it, they never "really seriously"
considered not having children. They believed that having
children is a fulfillment, that married couples who do not
have children are selfish and self-centered, and that couples
who do are healthier in mind.

JOE: I think having children is a fulfillment. . . . People that are married and don't have children tend to get more selfish as they get
older. And I think there's a lot of truth in that.

JENNIFER: If you see people without children, they tend to be very
selfish, self-centered people.

JOE: I think people who have children tend to be more outgoing, and
have a healthier attitude toward life.

They also believed the child would bring them closer to each
other.

JOE: I think it's going to pull us together more. . . . Each and every
little item that you do together or can discuss together or have
in common brings you closer together.

In addition to these reasons, the couple offered yet another reason why they opted for now. They wanted to start
a family before Jennifer got "too ambitious" in her job. The
fact is that while Joe might have just been starting his career,
Jennifer had become quite established in hers. She had become the supervisor of the bookkeeping department in the
company she had been working for since they were married.

JENNIFER: I figured I better have one before I got too ambitious in
my job. I was getting a lot of promotions and I decided if I got

too ambitious I may not want children. I might get too involved in materials things.

And in another interview,

JENNIFER: There's a point in your life when you should have a family. . . . If you wait too long, you start to believe that money is more important than family life. I've seen that happen to some other people.

Joe and Jennifer's deemphasis of "material things" and their positive regard for "family life" was, to a large degree, an outgrowth of their religious beliefs. At the core of these beliefs was the notion that working is for personal fulfillment and not for the monetary rewards it may bring. Jennifer spoke of being a full-time mother, so I asked her whether she believed she would return to work. She assured me she would, that she would like to work as a consultant eventually, if only part-time. She felt it was important for her to pursue her career, that "in this day and age, you need more than just the family." It was apparent that Jennifer's concept of self was related to her career as well as to her family. So was Joe's. While Jennifer's ambitions were being stifled, Joe's ambitions were being raised. Jennifer once said that when her "quiet," "subdued" family first met Joe, they were "shocked" by his frankness. The impression the couple gave, however, when they spoke of the effect which moving from student to worker had on Joe was that he had lost some of his assertiveness in the interim. Through his work he was evidently regaining his independence and self-confidence.

JENNIFER: I think Joe is getting more independent. . . . He's been working well with all the business people he's been dealing with lately. He's getting more self confident. . . .

INTERVIEWER: Do you feel that Joe lacked self-confidence?

JENNIFER: I think that when you first get out of school you do. You're not used to being with business people. You're used to being with students.

INTERVIEWER: What do you think about your self-confidence, Joe?

JOE: I think I'm gaining more self-confidence. With more experience you know what to do.

Another self-confidence builder which Joe was involved with was studying for the certified public accountant (CPA) exams. He didn't want to be a CPA. He just wanted to pass the exam and, as he said, "stick my tongue out." (At whom? He did not say.) Jennifer also wanted him to take the exam so that he would be more flexible. If he did not like one job, he would be able to move to another with more ease.

The fact that both Joe and Jennifer's individual concepts of self were so related to their respective careers is particularly interesting. When the subject of arguing came up (I asked all the couples what they usually argued about), Joe and Jennifer said that the thing they argued about the most was accounting and bookkeeping. When I asked them why they argued so much about accounting and bookkeeping, it became apparent that they considered themselves, more or less, in the same business—the business of handling money— and that in this business they both had their own ideas. Actually, they seemed to approach the business from two different points of view. Joe, as an accountant, represented the abstract or theoretical viewpoint. Jennifer, as a book-keeper, represented the concrete or pragmatic view.

INTERVIEWER: Why do you think you end up arguing about it?

JENNIFER: I think that's something we both have our own ideas on.

JOE: Sometimes I'm inconsistent and she points it out. At other times her knowledge about the subject is not as high as mine, so I have to sort of educate her.

JENNIFER: I'm more accurate and he's more knowledgeable. Put it that way.

And later on,

JENNIFER: He's an accountant, and I'm a bookkeeper.

JOE: Yea, she's a bookkeeper. Bookkeepers can find errors, and accountants can make up systems and can decide how the systems can run or why, and the bookkeepers can find errors.

JENNIFER: Bookkeepers can correct accountants' mistakes.

The classic conflict—education vs. experience—seems to be at the root of their discussion. Despite what may appear to most of us as an intellectual exercise, the fact that Joe and Jennifer's individual concepts of self are so related to the money-handling business make their confrontations more than a diversion. They are, I believe, manifestations of the same conflict which had been going on between them since they met in high school—who dominates whom?

Given that the onset of pregnancy signaled a change in the work structure of the couple's marriage, one might also suspect that their perennial conflict would develop into some interesting power plays and parries. This is, in fact, essentially what happened. Joe may have rebelled against his father's attempt to exert control as the husband-father. There were, however, indications that Joe too would have liked to command Jennifer's respect and subordination because he too was now the man of the house.

JOE: Well, I'm a pure male chauvinist pig, and I'll admit it.

JENNIFER: Yea.

Joe's chauvinism, or more precisely his belief that he should dominate Jennifer because that is the way it should be, was often not as explicit as the above admission, but there was no mistaking its existence in some of Joe's other comments. For example:

JOE: I don't really discuss the pregnancy that much with others. I let Jennifer do all the discussing. . . . My background with the people in this area; the men just don't discuss pregnancy . . . we let the women take care of that.

JOE: It seems like there's a breakdown in roles, if you know what I'm getting at. It seems like all the women want to be coal miners all of a sudden. It seems to be the thing to do. My theory is: that the women would be better off to stay home and take care of the kids and take care of the social clubs and that sort of stuff. And the men go out and earn the money. . . . I think the basic problem with juvenile delinquency in this country is in that the man goes out and works, the woman goes out and works, and the children are left home.

Unfortunately for Joe, Jennifer would not buy his ideological theory on who dominates whom. But the byproduct of parenthood (Jennifer leaving her job and Joe becoming the breadwinner) offered Joe another justification—resources. Resource theorists, you will recall,[1] contend that the allocation of tasks and power in a marriage is based on the comparative resources of the husband and wife. Within the resource theory system, Joe's claim to power would be structurally grounded on the assertion that he was bringing in what many couples consider the most important resource—money. Perhaps Jennifer tried to use this justification to dominate Joe during the first three and a half years of their marriage. She was then the breadwinner. And perhaps Joe, though he literally fought her attempts during the early years of their marriage to make such a claim,[2] eventually was convinced of her definition of the situation. Would this explain his loss of self-confidence which getting a job (resources?) helped him to regain? Whether or not Joe was making a claim based on rules which had existed all along, it was obvious that he anticipated using what he saw as his comparatively greater resources to support his domination. With the transition to parenthood he would become the breadwinner, he would have the responsibilities, and he would be in charge . . . or so he hoped.

JOE: I'm sort of proud and happy now that my wife's pregnant and we're going to have a child, and it was the motivating force in terms of me thinking about being the breadwinner, assuming a specific role. She's going to be staying home. Before, I was just another person going out and working and now I'm going to be the breadwinner. . . .

INTERVIEWER: Do you like that?

JOE: I think it's nice to feel that you're taking charge. . . . When you have responsibilities, you end up being in charge.

Once again, to Joe's frustration, Jennifer would not buy his theory on who dominates whom. She made it clear a number of times during the interviews that she had no intention of endorsing Joe's claim. The sequence which follows illustrates Joe's moves and Jennifer's countermoves in their negotiation of power.

INTERVIEWER: In the organization of your marriage, are you the boss?

JOE: In the circumstances here, in the way we're dividing the authority, now she's going to be the housewife and I'm going to be the principal breadwinner. That moves me up a notch in terms of being the breadwinner and having the say in financial matters. She's going to be in control of the house exclusively. She's going to have more say in what goes on with it, even more so with the furnishings of the house.

JENNIFER: I don't think he's the boss, because I never thought of myself as being the boss either.

INTERVIEWER: What do you think of Joe's notion that if he's making the money, he's a notch up on you?

JENNIFER: Oh, that's his idea.

JOE: Well, I think when . . . anybody does something to assume responsibility in a specific area, there is sort of a raising of him there in authority in that area. That's all I'm trying to get at. Because I will be the sole breadwinner, my authority will go up slightly.

INTERVIEWER: So your authority is going up here and Jennifer's is going to down here. [I motioned with my hands to indicate two different levels.]

JENNIFER: I'd still work on that one. . . . It's still going to work that mine will go up there. [Translation: I will still have as much authority as he has.] He thinks that way [but I know better].

INTERVIEWER: Do you believe he's the boss because he's the breadwinner?

JENNIFER: He can believe it if he wants.

INTERVIEWER: What do you think he believes?

JENNIFER: I think he's more of a householder. That's a better word.

JOE: Yea. I get stepped upon! [Laughter] . . . for example, if there should be a prowler in the house and they had a gun, I would probably assume responsibility in that circumstance because I'm in charge of the weapons, and I'm the more physical, violent personality! [Laughter] So I would take more responsibility in that circumstance because I am more knowledgeable. Now if she was gung-ho on guns, I'd say, "Here, you go downstairs. . . . [Laughter] That sort of thing. In times of emergency I take over. . . . We each assume our responsibilities in our own area.

INTERVIEWER: But you're going to be head of the household.

JOE: Yea. [Laughter] I like the way you said that!

INTERVIEWER: What does it mean to be head of the household?

JENNIFER: It means nothing. [Laughter]

JOE: This is what it means. It means nothing, but when a job is botched up, the buck stops here. That's what it means! [Laughter] . . . What I'm saying is if I'm the sole breadwinner, I think over a period of time I'll be feeling more authority in specific areas due to the circumstance that I'm familiar with. If she should get a job, my responsibility as sole breadwinner would have to go down. And hers will start to rise. She's the one who's going to be in contact with the kid more time than I am, so I'm going to have to lean over and say, "OK, she's the boss when it comes to taking care of and making decisions about this little kid." See what I'm getting at? Because this turns the area of responsibility, because she's more in touch with it, and so on and so forth. So what happens is that there are many areas of responsibility. So at any given point in time, you assume "boss of the car," "boss of the weapons," "boss for home defense," "boss for being breadwinner," "boss for heavy manual labor," "boss for repairs and replacements," "boss over the tools." Her—"boss for childrearing, food, shopping, household decisions." . . . I was just trying to explain that because I am earning the money solely that I probably will end up having more decision making power in that area.

JENNIFER: Yea, but I know how to handle it more.

There are a number of things worth noting in the above sequence. First of all, Joe's claim is bound to run into trouble from the start. He is attempting to argue that since he is the breadwinner, he is to have "the say" in financial matters. Given their sensitivity to money handling, Jennifer's final reply, "Yea, but I know how to handle it [money] more [because I'm a bookkeeper and you're an abstract accountant]," is predictable. Secondly, although Joe elaborates on his claim by arguing that responsibility implies authority, and that Jennifer will, because of her responsibilities, be "boss" of some areas too, the fact is some areas have more weight than others. The area in this household which carries the most weight is the financial area. Joe knows this, but then so does Jennifer. She refuses to give Joe's claim validity by denying it access to their world of consensual rules ("Oh, that's his idea." . . . "He can believe it if he wants." . . . "It means nothing.").

Toward the end of the pregnancy, it appeared that Joe had not given up on an ideological claim to power, that he in fact would resort to both ideology and resources to support his power play. By the fourth interview, Jennifer had quit work and was trying to adapt to being a housewife. It was difficult for her. She took a great deal of pride in the work she had done, the books she had set up, the department she supposedly had straightened out. When she left, everything started to "fall apart." The person who took Jennifer's place was having some problems making the transition, and as a consequence Jennifer had been called a number of times to give assistance over the phone. In spite of Jennifer's attachment to her previous job, Joe wanted her to "let go." He was actually quite vehement about it.

JOE: If they call up here, I'm going to get on the phone and act like a
      father. And I'm going to tell them, "Hey, you'd better hold up
      now, and if you call once more, I'm going to punch you in the
      mouth." And I'm going to hang up on them. And I know they
      are going to bother her. I don't want that to happen.

Joe's threats are significant. He says, first, that he is going
to "act like a father." Is it his father he is going to act like,
his father the patriarch who made all the decisions for Joe?
Second, he says that he is going to punch Jennifer's former
coworkers in the mouth. But who is he really threatening—
Jennifer's former coworkers or Jennifer herself?

Joe once stated that he felt the pregnancy made him more
of a man and Jennifer more of a woman. Perhaps what he
meant by this is that finally he can draw the line as his father
drew the line. Whether Jennifer can continue to resist re-
mains to be seen.

NOTES

1. The resource theory and ideological theory of marital power were first
outlined in the Daryl and Debby case study.

2. Speaking of how resources are used in the marital power struggle, Joe's
use of violence during the first two years of the marriage is perhaps a good illustration of how violence may be used as a resource. "[T] he willingness and ability
to use physical violence is a 'resource' in the Blood and Wolfe (1960) sense. A
family member can use this resource to compensate for lack of such other resources as money, knowledge, and respect. Thus, when the social system does not
provide a family member with sufficient resources to maintain his or her position
in the family, violence will tend to be used by those who can do so" (Steinmetz
and Straus, 1974: 9). At the time of the incident, Joe was a student and was
"behind" Jennifer in two important resources—income and occupational status.
Lacking these, did Joe fall back on his "ace in the hole"—his physical strength?

Chapter 5

LLOYD AND LINDA

For Lloyd and Linda, the first pregnancy and impending parenthood marked a phase in a transition which they had been undergoing since the day they decided to get married. The transition for them involved a revolution of ideas and behavior—a return from their sojourn into another world. The other world I am referring to is the world of the student activist in the late 1960s. Throughout each of the interviews one central theme continued to emerge. Lloyd and Linda were troubled by the fact that they were being pulled back to the world they knew before they went to college, the world in which they were raised, the world they fought against "in the riotous sixties." Lloyd and Linda were coming home to a middle-class way of life.

In September 1968, Lloyd and Linda each left the sanctuary of their homes to live away at college. Sometime during their freshman years they met, and soon thereafter decided to set up house. They continued to live together until their wedding at the beginning of their senior years. Lloyd described their premarriage relationship.

LLOYD: . . . very peculiar. . . . It wasn't like we were madly in love with each other, or something like that. We were just together. You know when you're an undergraduate in college, you're really fucked up anyhow. So on top of all this, we had this relationship. We didn't go out with anybody else.

While in college, Lloyd and Linda also became involved with the student movement. On a concrete level, their participation in the movement involved demonstrating against the domestic and foreign policies of the United States. On a more abstract level, and from their point of view, their participation meant that they had developed a cognitive frame of reference which was at odds with the frame of reference they had been taught at home. During the first interview they presented a picture of a marriage which was based on what they saw as an anti-middle-class theme.

INTERVIEWER: What type of marriage do you want to avoid?

LINDA: Nice middle-class.

LLOYD: You know, what your parents want you to be. Raise your kids. Come home from work every night and that's it.

LINDA: Stay home with the kids. Do club work, organizational work. That's what I want to try to avoid.

LLOYD: I think if we can maintain our individual interests and goals, to a large extent, we can avoid something like that.

Each time they described their ideal concept of marriage, they used their parents' marriages as a negative referent. Even Lloyd's last comment on individuality is an implicit dig against his parents.

LLOYD: My father—

LINDA: —can't exist without—

LLOYD: —would stand in the middle of the room for twenty-four hours without my mother. He just wouldn't move.

LINDA: He can't exist without her, which is bad.

During the second interview, they tried to illustrate again how their marriage was different from their parents'. The focus once more was individuality.

LINDA: I never, if someone asks my name, I never say Mrs. Lloyd L. I always say Linda L. I don't go around telling people I'm married, you know.

LLOYD: That's one of those things that's different from my parents.

LINDA: . . . Because I want to be known as myself, not as his right arm.

Despite their attempts to establish distance from their parents, one fact continued to emerge. Their behavior contradicted their ideal. Outwardly their marriage was, stereotypically, middle-class. They owned their own home, had a dog and two cars (one of which was a station wagon). They may have thought it was bad to have Lloyd "come home from work every night and that's it," but, in fact, that was Lloyd's pattern. Linda belonged to a bridge club and intended to "stay home with the kids." As far as their individuality, both preferred to watch TV together rather than be with their individual friends. If they were in the house, they considered it "important" that they be in the same room so they could be in each other's physical presence. Lloyd couldn't bear the idea of Linda not coming to bed with him at the end of the day. He would be extremely angry if Linda wanted to stay up and watch TV or read a book. Coming to bed with him was, he said, "one of the demands" he made on Linda. Loyd worked in his father-in-law's business. Linda wouldn't think of moving away from her folks. She wanted to see them at least once a week.

Lloyd and Linda were not oblivious to the contradictions they were living. In fact, trying to understand what happened was very much a part of their everyday existence. Having been members of the movement, how could they have ended up where they were? Lloyd speculated on one theory:

LLOYD: The problem that has always bothered me, as far as the kids who went to school in the late sixties, has never been resolved. None of us know yet. Were we, in the riotous sixties, what we really were, or are we getting to it now, becoming middle-class people? Because we all were children of middle-class homes. How much effect does it have on us?

Even though they were away at college, were they really away from being middle-class? Could any of them escape the fact that their proletarian way of life was made possible because their parents were supporting them? Were they really free, or were they simply given a longer leash which permitted them to believe they were straying? Lloyd and Linda's retrogression (their degeneration—as they saw it—to the middle-class way of behaving and, finally, thinking) did not take place immediately upon graduation. Rather the change was gradual, spanning at least three years. At the time of the pregnancy, their conversion back to the world of the middle class was in its last phases. It was here, given the contradiction that existed between their thoughts and behavior, that they began to conform their beliefs to their acts. In fact, the pregnancy itself was a strategy mutually directed to remove the last chance they may have had to recover.

The first step in the retrogression can be traced back to Christmas 1970. It was Linda's mother who made the first tug on the leash.

LLOYD: This is typical of her relationship with her mother. Even though she was away at school, Linda could not lie to her mother. It would upset her emotionally and get her very uptight. And one day we were home for Christmas vacation at my mother's house and her mother called Linda and she said to her, "Well, Lloyd will give you an engagement ring for a Christmas present." So Linda came and told me that, and we were sitting around and we had nothing else to do so I said, "Let's go down and buy an engagement ring." Just like that. And then that night we brought the ring home to my parents and showed it to them, and they said, "Oh, that's really nice." And then they went into their bedroom and closed the door, and stayed in there for about five hours [exaggeration?], and then they came out screaming, and they realized we were getting married. And then it dawned on Linda and I that we were going to get married. And Linda started to cry [Laughter]. We didn't go about it to get married. And then her father called me and talked to me for the first time in his life after three years.

Lloyd and Linda viewed their marriage as a concession to their parents. More importantly, they also saw it in retrospect as a turning point in their relationship. When they were living together their relationship was based on individuality and conflict with each other, patterns which they considered anti-middle class. Now that they were married they began to move toward togetherness and consensus.

LLOYD: We were together since 1968. So we were having a fight from day 1 of 1968. Then since we got married, we woke up the next morning and said, "What the hell did we get married for?" We started wending our way toward consensus, or, what's the word, acceptance, I guess. . . . Everything [was] completely turned around.

Perhaps Lloyd and Linda, in spite of the fact they were married, could have managed to have the anti-middle class relationship they so much wanted were it not for one fact: Linda's parents undermined the structure of their marriage by funneling them large amounts of money.

LLOYD: One of the problems with our marriage in the early years was the tug-of-war coming down heavy-handedly from her family. [Is Lloyd using the leash metaphor here?] Because they're the ones we lived near, and the ones that dish it out to us. Her father would say, "Here's a thousand dollars, have fun." And there are all these things, "Wait a minute, I've gotta work for my money. Why does he do that? I don't want to live like him."

In the beginning, Lloyd fought it. After a while, he just "accepted it."

LLOYD: When we bought this house, they came over and gave us a
    $5,000 check and we said, "Thanks," and I put it in the desk and
    went back to the bathroom. Just accepted it.

What does Lloyd mean when he says he "just accepted"
the $5,000? Does he mean that he had learned that it was no
use to try to fight it, that one way or another Linda's parents
would end up giving them the money no matter what he did
to resist? Or does he mean that he and Linda had become
more accepting of the middle-class way of life and that his
willingness to accept a check from his in-laws was a reflection
of their change in attitude? I believe that the second interpretation is more correct. This interpretation also raises the
question of what role did the injections of funds from Linda's
parents play in bringing about Lloyd and Linda's attitudinal
change? In effect, the money (a) created cognitive inconsistency for the couple, and (b) reinforced their middle-class
behavior.

Cognitive consistency theory asserts that people attempt
to perceive, cognize, or evaulate the various aspects of their
environments and of themselves in such a way that the behavioral implications of their perceptions shall not be contradictory (Deutsch and Krauss, 1965: 68). In short, people
need to believe that their cognitions are consistent—not dis-
sonant with one another. What the money did for Lloyd and
Linda was to create a life style of relative affluence which
was inconsistent with their conceptions of themselves as part
of the movement. In order to remove the dissonance, Lloyd
and Linda changed their conceptions of themselves to middle
class. Also operating was the reinforcing effect which the
money had. Instrumental learning theory (also called incen-
tive theory) asserts that attitudes become habitual because
their overt expression or internal rehearsal are followed by
the experience or anticipation of positive reinforcement
(Deutsch and Krauss, 1965: 90). In short, reinforced attitudes prevail. What the money also did for Lloyd and Linda
was to reinforce their overt expression of middle classness.

For example, as I will soon discuss, to Lloyd and Linda, buying a house is being middle class. The $5,000 which followed this act may be seen as a reinforcement. Perhaps Lloyd and Linda even bought the house in anticipation of the check!

The fact that Lloyd and Linda were more accepting of the gifts after they had bought their home is also significant because the purchase of their home was the second step in their retrogression. Before they lived where they now live, they rented an apartment. But (and Linda's parents may have realized this) apartment living was like being in college. At least this is how Lloyd and Linda saw their lives at that time. Apartment living provided the opportunity for them to maintain, to some extent, independence from each other. As Lloyd said, "We weren't really married."

LLOYD: Nine months ago, when we lived in the apartments, it was really independent. There were like twenty couples. The girls did things together and the guys did things together. . . . It was an extension of dormitory living. We weren't really married. Well, we weren't middle-class-living-in-a-house.

Lloyd's last comment is noteworthy. It gives an insight into what having a house meant to him and Linda. Having a house meant being married which meant being middle class. Once they were in their house, the independence which they had from each other "slowed down," according to Lloyd. Once they had their house, they were also on the track toward finishing (according to their conceptions) the middle-class picture—having kids. In fact, one of the reasons they gave for having a child was that they had a house! During the first interview, I asked why they decided to have the baby when they did. The first answer was that Linda could not find a job that she liked. Later on in the interview, Linda admitted that was not "really" the reason. She seemed unable to come up with a reason which she could classify as her own. She finally concluded that she must have decided to have a baby because Lloyd wanted it so badly.

LINDA: I don't know why I decided to. It was all up to me because
he had already made up his mind he wanted a child. He was
ready. It was all up to me. Why did I decide I wanted one? I don't
know. I mean I don't know what caused me to change my mind
all of a sudden. I think knowing that Lloyd wanted it so badly.

When we turn to Lloyd to find out why he wanted to have
a child, we are told that the house made him do it.

LLOYD: We always knew when we had the house, we would start to
think about it.

LLOYD: . . . This house is too big for two people.

LLOYD: I think what happened may be the rushing up of the baby
came along with the pushing up of my career . . . everything got
pushed back. . . . So I guess I condensed the baby too. We got
the house and, all of a sudden, a lot of things came too quickly
after we got the house. I figured, well, it's OK to have a kid now
and that's what brought the baby on.

Understanding how having a home would, for Lloyd, imply
parenthood requires understanding that Lloyd went through
life with what he called his "game plan." During the first interview, Lloyd spoke of his plan.

LLOYD: Well, I'm a very, how would you say, compulsive person.

LINDA: Compulsive person.

LLOYD: I think I know what I want to do with my life every step of
the way, you know. I want a certain job. I want to make a certain
amount of money, I want to have a kid, I want to be this place in
my career, and all that. . . . I literally go to the bathroom according to schedule.

It was always part of Lloyd's game plan to have children
with his home. When I asked him if he was compulsive about
everything, he said that he was not compulsive about his
wife. He illustrated his point by saying he "didn't marry
Linda because it was part of his game plan." This may be true

(it appears marriage may have been part of his parents-in-law's game plan), however there seems to be some evidence to support the notion that one of the reasons why Lloyd and Linda decided to have a child was that, according to Lloyd's timetable, they were due.

Lloyd's compulsiveness about life may have been a factor which predisposed him to accept more readily the money which was given to them by Linda's parents. There is a strong possibility that Lloyd's drive made it easier for him to accept a job in his father-in-law's company. Taking the job, and the salary which came with it, made it possible for Lloyd and Linda to buy their home and therefore be removed from the unmarriage type of life they had when they were in the apartments. And where did Lloyd get such motivation? Lloyd credits it to his upbringing.

LLOYD: I was raised that there were only two kinds of people in the world: those on top and those on the bottom. And you've got to be on top and that's all there is to it.

By taking the job with his father-in-law, Lloyd had, in the vernacular of the late 1960s, sold out. In spite of the rhetoric and accoutrements of the movement, deep down Lloyd was a nice middle-class boy. Perhaps no one realized this more than Lloyd. He considered it both the major flaw and the only stable thing in his life. His contradictory feelings toward himself were projected in his attitude toward his parents-in-law. He both hated and loved them for what they had done to him and for him. Nowhere in the transcripts is Lloyd's paradoxical relationship with himself and his in-laws more apparent than in a sequence which took place during the second interview. During that interview, while we were talking about Linda's parents, the phone rang and Lloyd answered it. It was Linda's mother. The sequence which follows includes not only the phone conversation but also the conversation before and after.

INTERVIEWER: Do you feel the problem with Linda's mother will be changed when the baby comes?

LLOYD: No, it's just a standoff and I'm sure once again that I will lose, and compromise, and let them talk and take the kid to spoil it to [big city] and there'll be nothing I can do. After the baby's born, they'll move in a roomful of furniture or two. I'll just accept it. I'll tell Linda I'll fight it, but I won't.

INTERVIEWER: Is that what you object to, the fact that they would do something like that?

LLOYD: Yes, because they do that with everything. They've compromised a little bit, but I've compromised more than they have.

LINDA: Yes. Everybody's compromised a little. Not as much as you have.

LLOYD: They've compromised with their mouth. They don't say much. They just mail it over now. [What? The money?] ... But they're afraid I'm going to bite them, which is all I've got now, and they think twice before they talk.

LINDA: I don't think my mother is going to butt in much.

LLOYD: She will.

LINDA: You think so?

LLOYD: In her self-affixing way. But this is something I can say, this is my territory. I can really put my foot down. Although I thought I could do that when it came to my house. I don't dare throw them out. I tell them to shut up. There's nobody else that I've ever been quiet for.

TELEPHONE: Ring ... Ring ...

LLOYD: Oh, we were just talking about you! Oh, only complimentary things.

LINDA: It must be my mother [addressed to Interviewer].

LLOYD: Ha! Ha! Ha! Behind your back is your chair, I'm sure. We have our shrink over here with us—the guy doing the survey on the marriage.

LINDA: The marriage? It's on pregnancy!

LLOYD: The pregnancy, that's what it's all about. [Pause.] Very good. Bye.

TELEPHONE: Clunk.

LLOYD: See how polite I was.

LINDA: Yes.

LLOYD: She said, "You're lying. You're not saying nice things."

LINDA: She knows you don't like her.

LLOYD: Does she? Why, did she ever tell you that?

LINDA: No, I can tell.

LLOYD: Why, because she never kisses me?

LINDA: She has once.

LLOYD: Once, on our wedding day. Do you really think she thinks I don't like her?

LINDA: Yes.

Noteworthy are the contradictions: (a) Lloyd first states that his in-laws are afraid of him, that they fear he might "bite them," that he can tell them to "shut up." Then he confesses that "there's nobody else that I've been quiet for." (b) He also implies that he is the master of his own home, that it is "his territory." He admits, however, that he could never "throw his in-laws out," though he thought evidently at one time that he could. (c) In spite of the hatred he projects before and during the phone call, after he hangs up he becomes very concerned that his mother-in-law might know he doesn't like her.

During the year before the pregnancy, Lloyd's repugnance to the fact that he was dependent on his in-laws for his living was beginning to outweigh the attraction having such a position held for him. Lloyd started to lean toward recovery. That is to say, he was threatening to quit work and return to school in order that he might make it on his own. The pregnancy, as far as they were concerned, stifled any chances they might have had to cut the leash. It essentially marked the third step in the retrogression. During the second interview, I asked again why they decided to have a baby at the time they did. A new reason emerged, one which demonstrates that Linda was not simply an onlooker to the retrogression but that she and Lloyd were codirectors of their self-proclaimed tragedy.

LINDA: I know another reason why I did it. I can't say it in front of you, Lloyd. Lloyd comes home every night, and says, "I'm leaving my job, I'm going back to school." And I'm a bit afraid of him quitting. Now it comes out.

LLOYD: No kidding, I knew that.

LINDA: I'm a little bit afraid of him quitting. I don't know why, I guess because of the security that I have now. So I figured that if I had a kid, he wouldn't leave. Too late now, hon.

LLOYD: Boy, you're sneaky. You're rotten! That's a terrible reason to have a child.

LINDA: But I was so worried.

The pregnancy was, to use a cliché, the point of no return. Once they knew they were going to be parents, Lloyd and Linda's return to the world of the middle class became a foregone conclusion. Over the course of the pregnancy period, I was able to monitor the next to final phase in their transition. By comparing comments made across the four interviews, I was able to note significant changes in their behavior and in their way of thinking, changes which would ease them into the fourth (and possibly final) step in the retrogression—parenthood.

During the first interview, Lloyd and Linda's concept of marriage was based on a philosophy of personal freedom. Lloyd talked about his Saturday morning breakfasts with the guys. Linda spoke of her plans to take a pack horse trip across the country the following summer. Their descriptions of what they did *not* want their marriage to be reflected everything their parents' marriages were. As noted, during this interview Linda brought up the fact that she could not get a good job and that that might have influenced her to have a child now. When I asked her if she intended to stay home when the baby arrived, she was quick to point out that she had no intention of remaining a housewife for the rest of her life, that, yes, she had every intention of trying to find work, if only part time. Lloyd also revealed his "game plan" during this interview. At the time of the first interview, they were about to buy a new car. Linda said they refused to buy a station wagon, something she equated with a middle-class way of life.

Symbolic perhaps is the fact that when I came for the second interview, I was told that they *had* bought a station wagon! They said they could not believe what was happening to them. (Yes, *to* them. They gave the impression that they felt they were not responsible for their changes.) Lloyd said that his "game plan" had become "less urgent," that he was becoming, to use his words, "an amorphous mass of middle classdom." Linda's trek across the country had, in a sense, also become less urgent. Whereas before she considered the trip an example of her independence, now she was worried about geographical hazards and being lonely. Perhaps the most significant change to be noted since the first interview was their withdrawing from many of their college friends. They said they "just didn't get along with them anymore." They were a little annoyed that their friends would not stick with them through the changes they were going through. They defined "a friend" as someone who would be willing to stick by you no matter what, implying that they felt they were going through a crisis in their lives. The rift between Lloyd and Linda and their former friends is important because it removed the couple from the student movement reference group. A reference group is that group which serves as the point of reference in making comparisons and contrasts, especially in forming judgements about one's self, and/or that group in which the actor aspires to gain or maintain acceptance, and/or that group whose perspective constitutes the frame of reference of the actor (Shibutani, 1955). Losing touch with the student movement reference group meant losing the reinforcement they would have needed to fight the transition. Perhaps those friends with whom they did get along were the marginal members of the group. Maybe Lloyd and Linda with these others now constituted a new reference group, a group which would construct a new (middle-class? semi-middle-class?) frame of reference, a group which would come together to define their former group as not really friends, as outsiders.

Accompanying their cutting themselves off from their friends was their growing dependence on each other. They mentioned that they liked to stay home more. When I asked what they thought about the fact that they were spending more and more time with each other, they said that they believed their marriage was stronger, that they liked each other more. Later, however, in the same interview they classified their situation as "sickening."

LLOYD: I'm really turning inward. I'm giving up a lot of things.

LINDA: Gee, I hope it changes by the time you're here next time! It's sickening.

LLOYD: It sure is.

Lloyd and Linda's ambivalence toward their marriage, I believe, is indicative of their transition. Although they were outwardly becoming what they saw as middle class, inwardly (cognitively) they had not yet made the transition. Lloyd made this very point in the second interview.

LLOYD: Well, maybe outwardly, we still live like our parents did, or do. But there's certainly been a thought process that was tremendously different. Our thoughts, for instance, about the role of women in the world is totally different than our parents' conceptions. Perhaps we make Linda function like our parents do, but we still conceive that there is a viable alternative. We don't put people down for living alternatively, so we're aware of it. We've put some thought into it. We've made a progression of thought. I just don't know if we've exhibited it too much.

Actually, their "thought process" was showing some signs of change during the interview. In addition to their positive evaluation of their marriage ("more stable," "we like each other better"), they also noted some change in their attitudes toward what they considered pivotal issues—abortion and divorce.

LLOYD: We were discussing it the other night. Of course, we were always proabortion. We said we could never have an abortion now.

LINDA: Gee, I can't believe I said that.

INTERVIEWER: You can't believe you said which one?

LINDA: That I can't see abortion anymore. I wouldn't do it myself.

INTERVIEWER: And you can't believe you said it now?

LINDA: Yes, when I was so proabortion a few years ago.

INTERVIEWER: What made you change your mind?

LINDA: When I got pregnant!

LLOYD: But now I think I could sacrifice for the kid, almost to the extreme of staying together.

INTERVIEWER: So you would stay together?

LINDA: Unless it was really bad. Probably.

INTERVIEWER: But you could conceive of it now?

LINDA: I could conceive of it, sure.

LLOYD: We used to say that's ridiculous.

LINDA: Yes.

When I returned for the third interview, Lloyd and Linda's retrogression was becoming more and more an inevitable turn of events. Given the ambivalence they felt during the second interview, it could be argued (assuming the validity of cognitive consistency theory previously discussed) that they had one of two options open to them. Either they could change their behavior to conform to their beliefs, or they could change their beliefs to conform to their behavior. In effect, they were locked into their middle-class behavioral pattern by their bank account, their home, Lloyd's executive position, and the pregnancy. Given that changing their behavior pattern was highly unlikely, their beliefs began to retrogress. Gone was the classification of their way of life as "sickening."

LLOYD: Well, I think I told Linda the other day, that I feel a little more content with myself right now.

INTERVIEWER: What makes you say that?

LLOYD: I'm at ease . . . I'm happy and I have no ambition. [Lloyd's use of the word "ambition" here refers to the "game plan" he set for himself in college. He often used the term in this context.]

INTERVIEWER: What do you think of Lloyd's changes?

LINDA: Oh, I think they're nice. He has changed I guess. . . . He likes to stay home and do nothing.

INTERVIEWER: Do you like that?

LINDA: Yes.

INTERVIEWER: What was it like before?

LINDA: He always liked to go out, go out and play. Now he's more content to stay home.

Lloyd's attitude toward his work took an interesting turn. He spoke now of how his father-in-law was beginning to appreciate him more, how he had proved himself as a capable executive. He reflected on the past, on how his in-laws had tried at one time to "boost him out" (come between him and Linda) but that now they were beginning to almost realize that "Linda was very lucky" to have married him.

LLOYD: She [Linda's mother] likes me this month.

INTERVIEWER: How do you know that she likes you this month?

LLOYD: Because we spent the weekend at the chalet with them. Almost to the point that they realized that Linda was very lucky to get married to me, that she really has an outstanding marriage.

INTERVIEWER: Is this about the closest they've come?

LLOYD: Oh yea. Along way back they were boostin' me out. Now she's almost to the point that she respects that I am the boss of my own household. It has a lot to do with the fact I work with my father-in-law, which is a very confusing situation. First my father-in-law and his partner took me on because Linda and I needed money. "Give the kid a job." In the last month or two [however] they have come to realize that not only could I do my job. They had me come into his office and they said, "You know, we actually have the belief that maybe someday you could come to sit in this chair." They never thought anybody else could. In other words, I'm not just on the payroll because I'm a son-in-law. They believe I can do a job, maybe better than some of the other junior jerk executives.

Lloyd implies in the above series that his father-in-law finally discovered Lloyd's worth with the firm. Another possibility is that Lloyd finally came around to their way of thinking, and their approval of him is an indication not of their discovering what had been there all the while, but of Lloyd's compliance.

A critical aspect in Lloyd and Linda's transition was their reconstruction of their marital and personal identities (their conception of who they were together and individually). At the end of the third interview, Lloyd and Linda concluded that "deep down" they were very traditional inside, and that they had known this all along. The fact that they claimed they "always" knew it is important because it signifies a reconstruction of not only their present conceptions but a reconstruction of their former conceptions as well. Thus they had created a common past which permitted them to view what was happening to them as not simply inevitable, but, according to Lloyd, a return to "the only content part of life." Being traditional "deep down" meant that now they assessed their retrogression as a return to stability and continuity. They were coming home.[1]

It is important to note that Lloyd and Linda's transition was continuous and not discrete. By that I mean their transition from the student world to the middle class world was not a sharp or complete transition from one world to the next. Rather, it would be better to conceptualize the retrogression as a movement on a continuum in which the student world and the middle-class world are poles. Thus, once Lloyd and Linda became students in 1968 and participated in the movement soon thereafter, they did not completely divorce themselves from their middle-class world. Had they done so, the Christmas phone call from Linda's mother, in which she predicted that Lloyd would buy Linda an engagement ring, would not have the effect that it did. So also, their retrogression to the middle-class world did not mean that they had completely removed themselves from the student world of which they were once a part. What *was* taking place through each of the steps in the retrogression was that Lloyd and Linda's position on the continuum was changing. With each step they moved closer to the middle-class pole. Perhaps, in time, their position on the continuum will be so close to the middle-class pole that the student world will have little, if any, effect.

During the fourth interview, we talked about their plans for when the baby arrived. Both agreed that having the child would be the "final cement" between them, that it would "tie them together" and that their marriage would be "stronger" (less likely to end in divorce?). Linda talked of "finding something" to do because she could not see herself "just sitting around" with the child. When I asked if she intended to go back to work, she said that she did not know, that work was not important, and that she would probably find some "volunteer work."

INTERVIEWER: Do you intend to go back, Linda?

LINDA: I don't know. If I could find a good full-time job, I certainly wouldn't mind working full time.

INTERVIEWER: Is it important to you that you work?

LINDA: No.

INTERVIEWER: What do you see yourself doing as the child grows to pass the time?

LINDA: I don't know. Something. I'll find something.

INTERVIEWER: Like what?

LINDA: Volunteer work, tending to the household. I can't see myself just sitting around.

It is remarkable that Linda mentioned that she would be willing to find volunteer work. During the first interview, when I asked her what type of marriage she and Lloyd wanted to avoid, she responded, "Nice middle class. . . . Stay home with the kids. Do club work, organizational work. That's what I want to try to avoid."

Lloyd reiterated the position he took during the third interview, saying, "I think secretly we've harbored the basic marriage beliefs." He also mentioned for the first time his "home office," a room in the house set aside evidently just for Lloyd. He spoke of his office as a place where he could "think about all the things he was going to be"—his game plan, his ambitions.

INTERVIEWER: Do you like having this private room to yourself?

LLOYD: Yes, it's great. I think about all the things I was going to be. . . .

LINDA: I know. You can do whatever you want to do in there.

Lloyd's office was a memories room, an altar to a (forever lost?) dream. It was all that was left of "the riotous sixties." Parenthood (the fourth stage) was less than a month away.

NOTE

1. For a discussion of identity construction, past and present, see Berger and Luckmann (1966). For a discussion of the issue within the context of marriage, see Berger and Kellner (1964).

Chapter 6

A CONFLICT APPROACH TO

MARRIAGE: Presuppositions

The purpose of the next two chapters is to answer the general questions originally posed: How does the husband-wife system work during the first pregnancy? How does the husband-wife system work in general? The chapters are a combination of previous research findings, existing theories, and insights gleaned not only from the four case studies but from the total sample. The basic theme of these synthesis chapters is, to some extent, implied in the case studies. After the four in-depth analyses were written, I asked myself, "How do the cases differ from each other and how are they similar?" The answer I arrived at is that the common thread which ties the four couples together is conflict, and the differences which each of the couples exhibits are variations on a conflict theme.

Daryl and Debby illustrate this theme in their differences over whether their activities should be complementary (activities of husband and wife are different and separate but fitted together to form a whole), independent (activities are carried out separately without reference to each other, in so far as this is possible), or joint (activities are carried out together, or the same activity is carried out by either partner at different times).[1] Hank and Helen's conflicts stem from their differences over whether their marriage should be based on the principle of fusion ("becoming one") or on individuality. Joe and Jennifer's perennial debate is "who shall dominate?" Lloyd and Linda are somewhat of a special case. First, most of their conflicts are between them and Linda's parents. Second, they are the only couple whose intrapersonal conflicts proved to be a major topic.

One point should be made clear: By "conflict" I do not mean that husbands and wives are necessarily always fighting with each other. Though marital conflict may sometimes escalate to heated arguments and physical violence, these activities are but two ways in which conflict may manifest itself. Essentially, what is being advanced in the next two chapters is the notion that the husband-wife relationship is better understood as a unit in which the actors are concerned primarily with the furthering of their own individual interests. In other words, rather than view marriage as a relationship built on consensus, the conjugal dyad is conceptualized as a system in which confrontation is inevitable and consensus is problematic (Sprey, 1969: 702).

Though a conflict approach to marriage is not a new idea, it is an idea which is at odds with the "common sense" conceptions of how marriage works. One might expect governments, prisons, or even universities to offer examples of social units riddled with conflict; but marriages? How is it possible to claim that the most intense and most valued interpersonal relationship in America today operates according to the conflict paradigm? In what is perhaps the most developed presentation on the conflict approach to family life, Sprey (1969) discusses a number of fallacies which he feels impede the realization that, at its core, the family is a conflict arena.

Since these fallacies serve to obscure the underlying causes of confrontation in marriage, Sprey's arguments are worth reviewing.

There is No Real Normative Alternative to the Married State as a Life Career

The first fallacy Sprey discusses is the belief that participation in the family is a voluntary matter. To dispute this claim, Sprey notes that membership in one's family of orientation is obviously not by choice, and that (more important to this discussion) there is no real normative alternative to the married state as a life career. With respect to the latter point, Sprey contends that marriage may be a "personal commitment" but it is "one made, consciously or unconsciously, under societal duress" (Sprey, 1969: 702).

But what about the increasing number of people opting for the single life, and the higher divorce rate? Do these changes not point to the existence of "alternatives"? These patterns do suggest that marriage is becoming more "voluntary." Still, less than 10 percent of the United States' population never marry, and over 80 percent of all married persons in America have been married only once (Schulz, 1976: 146, 212). Evidently, the social norm to marry and remain married, though perhaps changing, is still strong.

In order to gain some understanding of the subjective aspects of "societal duress," I asked each of the sample couples why they decided to get married rather than remain single. Interestingly, only one couple was able to verbalize specific reasons for not remaining single.

PETER: I think it's just a person's nature to want to settle down. . . . I probably like to raise hell just as much as anybody else, you know, chasing women and so on, but you just can't do that, you know, for sixty years. I mean there's just something inside you that says that's not what I was put here for.

PAMELA: . . . you don't want to live with your parents all your life, and neither of us could live alone I don't think. . . . I guess all you

hear about, you know, grow up and get married. And I guess you're
brought up with that ideal that that's what you're going to do.

All of the other couples gave answers more or less similar
to Joe and Jennifer's—"someplace along the line" it was just
assumed. The social norm of marrying had apparently been
internalized so well that marriage was just taken for granted.

Few couples, on the other hand, had difficulty responding
to a question on cohabitation. Given the option between
marrying or just living together the couples were more cog-
nizant of "outside pressure."

INTERVIEWER: Why did the two of you decide to get married? Why
didn't you just live together?

AMY: [Religious] bringing up. I think it would have hurt our families
too much. My mother would die there right on the spot. She
could never adjust to it.

ALAN: ... It [living together] is not me.

IRENE: I wouldn't live together. I wouldn't live with anybody because
my parents wouldn't like that. Well, I wouldn't. I wouldn't do
anything to hurt them. I was living at home until we got married.... Living together never really entered my, did it enter
your mind? It never entered mine.

IKE: No. We might have talked about it in passing, but I don't think
on a serious note.

BARBARA: In 1965 [the year of their marriage] that was a no-no.
My upbringing—

BRAD: Before we were married, your parents wouldn't let us go out
on the island. And I don't think you considered it for even three
seconds.

NANCY: I don't know ... society accepts married couples where they
don't accept people living together.

And when the discussion turned to the level of commitment which marriage vs. living together entails, the absence

of alternatives to the married state was shown even more clearly. A number of the couples assumed that marriage is a relatively permanent arrangement.

FRAN: The freedom. You still have freedom if you're just living together. You might say you love him, but if something happens you can walk out the door. You might think twice if you're married.

FITZ: [When you're married] you make vows to each other, promises to each other. Compared to living together: If I want to go out and have a beer and she says "No," well, she has no say.... Married, if I want to do something, I'll discuss it with her. If we're living together, if I want to do something, I'll do it. You're not tied down.

FRAN: You'll always have that thing over your head, "You don't own me."

GLORIA: [Living together] there's just that one little out. If we had an argument, it might be a little easier to walk out.... It just seems that you can get out of it more easily, and you might not try as hard.

INTERVIEWER: What do you think, George?

GEORGE: ...When you're married, there are no holds barred. You have committed yourself in law and, sooner or later, they're going to find out all the gory details.... There's no easy way out. If you find out that your husband wears weird socks, you can't pack up your stuff and walk.

NANCY: When you're just living together you can just get up and walk out anytime, no strings attached.

NORMAN: You can do that when you're married.

NANCY: Well, it's a little harder.

MARK: I think it [marriage] is not just a piece a paper. I think it's more than that; more like a bondage together.

INTERVIEWER: What do you have that you wouldn't have if you were living together?

MARIE: *Him.* If we had been just living together, I wouldn't *have* him.

The sequence by Mark and Marie is particularly interesting. When Marie says that if she and Mark were not married, she would not "have" Mark, she is referring to the fact that their first year of marriage was particularly rough and that if they were not in "bondage" (Mark's term) to each other by marriage, they would have gone their separate ways. Marriage, thus, permitted her to keep Mark. The connotation here is not simply imprisonment, it is enslavement—the same metaphor which Sprey uses in a later paper when he is discussing, once again, the lack of alternatives to marriage: "Sociologically speaking, the main 'enslaving' quality of marriage lies in the fact that there exists no real, and equal, alternative to it" (Sprey, 1971-2: 6).

PARENTHOOD AS A LIFE CAREER

In view of the fact that for a majority of Americans marriage implies raising children, it is important to realize that parenthood, like marriage, is a commitment made consciously or unconsciously under societal duress (see Peck, 1971; Peck and Senderowitz, 1974; Whelan, 1975). Despite the advances made in contraceptive techniques during the past decade, there is no real normative alternative to parenthood as a life career. Noting this, one may wonder how typical the comments of the sample couples are.

George and Fitz, for example, give the impression that not having children is "unfair."

GEORGE: There's going to be eight billion people on this planet, and everybody is allowed to have so many children. It would be unfair that we didn't have any and somebody else did, because we could offer our child so much, and his place might be taken by a "redneck" or something. I just think that we have a lot to give a child. Gloria carries along the traditional recipes, and things like that, and how to keep a clean house.

INTERVIEWER: Would you agree with people who got married and decided not to have any children?

FITZ: I can't see it myself. If they're able to have children, why not have them? There are people in the world who can't have kids, that would love to have kids. . . . When you come right down to it, they [people who decide not to have children] are depriving life.

Fitz's comment must be weighed against the remark he makes only moments before. He then was talking not about his responsibility to give life, but to demand life from his children when he is old.

FITZ: The way I feel, if we were unable to bear children, I would have to adopt. You figure when you get older, and you want to look back upon what you've done, I want to look back and see what I've done for my kids. You're not just going to grow old and be lonely. You'll have somebody. Like if something should happen to me, she [Fran] is going to have somebody to look after her, or whatever. She's not just going to be a stranger on the street, an old lady walking around town. She's going to have relatives. Because her folks and my folks won't be around forever. I mean it's going to end up that it's going to be loneliness, and I think that if a child can bring so much happiness, why deprive yourself? . . . Say if we never wanted any children, what would happen to me? If something were to happen to her, okay, what would happen to me? I'd end up like a town drunk, right? I wouldn't have anybody.

The children as a refuge theme was also advanced by one of the case study couples. Joe and Jennifer felt that children offer a sanctuary from marriage and work.

INTERVIEWER: What made you decide to have children?

JOE: I think you miss a lot by not having children.

JENNIFER: It's nice to have a home and all. After a while, when it's just the two of you it gets—

JOE: Yes, I think a marriage can get very dull.

JENNIFER: You can only find so much self satisfaction in your own job.

JOE: I think having children is a fulfillment.

In contrast to Joe and Jennifer, Ike argued that children *made* his marriage.

IKE: I think having children is one of the main motivations of getting married. It should be anyway. . . . The fact is our landlord has been married for almost twenty years now and has never had any children, never had any desire for children. I don't know whether she [the landlord's wife] did; that's none of my business. But to me, their marriage, other than being legally binding, has no bearing, no basis.

And Norman attributed his decision to his having to "live up to standards."

NORMAN: Once you get married you're supposed to live up to standards.

INTERVIEWER: What standards?

NORMAN: The people put out; people put standards out for other people. If they [a couple] get married they [the people] say, "Oh, they are going to stay together and have kids and everything, you know."

Norman's comment on the existence of a community attitude which he is compelled to follow is a good illustration of George Herbert Mead's (1934) concept of "generalized other." Many spouses also were able to name specific "others" whose standards had to be adhered to. Not surprisingly, the most intense pressure came from parents.

NORMAN: He's the only grandchild right now, the dog.

NANCY: We tease him [my father] about that, tell the dog, "Go see Grampy or Grammy," you know, tease him about it. My sisters don't have any kids.

NORMAN: When we go and visit somewhere he'll say, "Yes, I got a grandchild," and he'll tell them all about the dog and they'll look at him, you know. It's really funny.

GLORIA: My mother is the [European] mother, and I'm the oldest child, and I'm the first one married. And I think after the first year goes by, they start to worry about you. She's tried to be cool about it, but she's hinted that she'd like to be a grandmother. I called her up and said, "This is the phone call you've been waiting for for three years."

AMY: [Alan's mother] thought I should've stayed home and had children right away. When Alan told her I was pregnant, she said "It's about time!" She thinks your only purpose in life is to be married and have children.

FITZ: If it had been up to my folks, we would have had one before we were married.

Another set of "others" whose standards had to be lived up to were friends. The pressure here however seemed to be more self-imposed, more a function of "keeping up with the Joneses."

PETER: I think a lot of people feel that as soon as they're married then they should have a child. And we didn't feel that way. Because we felt that we got married to be together and we wanted to have some time married together, just her and I which we have had for two years—

PAM: It'll be almost three.

PETER: Almost three.

PAM: But now I feel we're kind of slow on getting started. You know you see all these girls that are still going to school and they've got, you know, two or three kids, and they're pretty old. You know, it makes me feel like I'm kind of late.

GEORGE: Statistically, if you were to interview people that were pregnant and ask them how many of their friends were pregnant in the previous two years, you'd find the incidence would be much higher than normal. . . .

GLORIA: We're the end of all of our friends who just had babies, you know, and I can definitely say for me too, you know, the more I saw my friends' babies, I wanted to know what mine was going to look like, you know, I was just getting more and more ready to start my own family. I could see it happening very definitely. . . . I think George saw it happening, too, the more everybody brought babies to our house, it was getting beyond me. You know, we made it for three years without one. Okay, you know, we'll start a family someday but with more babies we were surrounded by it and it became a very real possibility to us. It became something like all of a sudden I really wanted one.

Finally, like the social norm to marry, the social norm to parent can become internalized to the point that a couple is sometimes hard pressed to verbalize why they decided to have children. The best illustration of this is Daryl and Debby who admitted that they may have given more thought to whether or not to own a cat.

DARYL: I don't know whether we actually gave the cat more consideration.

DEBBY: I think we did. . . . We planned the arrival of the cat specifically so we'd get him just before we moved out of the house.

AMBIVALENCE IN MARRIAGE

Because marriage and parenthood are not actually "free choices," a feeling of ambivalence permeates the husband-wife relationship. Underlying this feeling are the perennial questions: "Do I (we) really want to be married?" "Do I (we) really want this child?" Brad, who had been married for nine years, disclosed his confrontation with the perennial "Why?"

BRAD: I don't have any good answers for "Why?" And it's not as easy as "because everybody does it, or because we wanted to." It's like, "Why did you get married? Why do you choose to do what you do?" . . . Be damned if I know why we decided to [start a family].

In some cases this feeling is denied, in others it is accepted. Denial is understandably difficult to assess. For example, are Owen and Olyvia denying their ambivalence toward parenthood in the following passage, or are they "really" pronatalistic?

OWEN: But there are people who the thought of having kids in the house just drives them crazy. They couldn't cope with it. I really do think that they are lacking something.

OLYVIA: I feel badly for them.

OWEN: Their whole world is centered around just two people, on themselves really. And I don't think that could be a good marriage either.

OLYVIA: But how can you put them down because they're happy?

OWEN: But are they really happy?

OLYVIA: That's the thing that you can't really measure because we're not them.

OWEN: . . . We can't really tell because we really want to have children.

OLYVIA: We can't understand them not wanting children.

OWEN: We would be lacking if we didn't.

One couple admitted openly that they felt uneasy about being married and making the transition to parenthood. This was Lloyd and Linda, a case study couple. They were not alone. Kevin conceded that at times he needed to escape. And Cheryl confessed to feeling trapped.

KEVIN: There are times . . . when I wish I could just forget this house, this existence. And sometimes I do it. I'll just walk around the block, and while I'm walking around, I try to shut everything out of my mind, just walk and not think anything. By the time I get back again, this place has become real again. So you might say, at that particular time, that I wished I was divorced of everything—the marriage, the house, everything.

CHERYL: I feel trapped by the baby a little, even though I want it. Already I'm worried about being stuck home all the time. That sounds funny because I'm not a career type person, but it does bother me a little bit, not being able to come and go if I want.

Evidently, the fact that a marriage or a pregnancy is "planned" does not mean that a couple is free from experiencing some apprehension over their "decision."

Marriage is a Transactional System

Another fallacy discussed by Sprey is the notion that the family is a buffer between the individual and society, that the family serves as a world into which one may withdraw from the conflicts of everyday life. In reply to this notion, Sprey asserts that the reverse could also be true. That is, it could also be argued that one way of escaping the conflicts of family life is to withdraw to the impartial and predictable world of everyday life. Both notions suffer from the misconception that the individual is "somehow apart from society, while moving more or less at will from one societal institution to another" (Sprey, 1969: 703). As an alternative to this conception, Sprey offers one in which "individuals participating in families, or whatever institutional arrangements, are seen as being involved in society itself" (Sprey, 1969: 703). The idea that the husband-wife relationship cannot be understood apart from the environment with which it transacts is a point made by a number of conflict theorists. Simmel, for example, discussed the significance of this transaction in terms of the couple's subjective experience:

No couple has by itself invented the form of marriage. Its various forms are valid, rather, within culture areas, as relatively fixed forms. . . . [I]n regard to its content and interest, as well as to its formal organization, this most personal relation of all is taken over and directed by entirely super-personal, historical-social authority. . . . Although each of the two spouses is confronted by only the other, at least partially he also feels as he does when

confronted by a collectivity; as the mere bearer of a super-individual structure whose nature and norms are independent of
him, although he is an organic part of it (Simmel, 1950: 130).

The "super-individual structure" to which Simmel refers
is of course the social structural and cultural context in which
a marriage is "located." In the past century in America, there
have been some radical changes in the environmental context,
and these have resulted in a transformation of the husband-
wife relationship. The major social structural change is industrialization (women can now better compete in the labor
market). The major cultural changes are the increased popu-
larity of individualism and sex role equalitarianism as ide-
ologies (both of which were causes and consequences of
industrialization), (Goode, 1963). The significance of these
changes with respect to the marital system is that they undermined the assumed legitimacy of the traditional marriage
arrangement in which husbands "naturally" lead and wives
"naturally" follow. The lower the legitimacy of a power
structure, the higher the perceived conflict of interests (Duke,
1976: 272).

> What industrial society does is to strike down the ancient irrever-
> sibilities of *ascribed* roles—those gotten by birth; and open up the
> possibility of *achieved* roles— those gotten by individual attain-
> ments. Until modern times, women received their major gratifica-
> tions or rewards by "pleasing" husband and children. There was,
> in that premodern setting, very little challenge or conflict to
> males and hence the status quo was maintained. . . . *Modern so-*
> *ciety provides the kinds of conditions under which women are*
> *able to challenge (conflict with) male privileges* (Scanzoni, 1972:
> 34).

It is important to recognize that modernization does not
create a conflict situation in the marital system, it simply
changes some of the rules of the game, thereby making the
confrontation more apparent. The strong patriarchal system
that existed before industrialization was an effective tool in

the exploitation and subjugation of women. The relatively passive manner in which the majority of women accepted their subordinate position is, from a conflict perspective, indicative of the degree to which women had been socialized (read brainwashed). The model of marriage as a confrontation of interests "fits" in both premodern and modern societies. In modern societies, however, the management of these conflicts is more problematic and thus more observable.

Marriage is a Paradox

Another important reason for approaching marriage as a system in conflict is the paradoxical nature of the husband-wife relationship. This point is not made by Sprey in his 1969 article. It is however implied in one of his later papers:

> A human bond . . . is a paradox. Moving closer to another person also, by necessity, means moving apart. That is, increasing intimacy brings with it an increasing awareness of, and confrontation with, the uniqueness of other. The more special two people become to each other the greater may be the pressure, from both sides to possess the other totally, or in popular phraseology, to "become one." And that indeed, would mean the end of reciprocity. Intimacy, to be viable, thus requires the awareness, and acceptance, of the stranger in the other (Sprey, 1971: 724).[2]

One of the central characteristics of contemporary American marriage is the high degree to which a husband and wife must depend on each other for emotional support. This is because, as a neolocal unit, contemporary marriage is a relatively isolated system (relative, that is, to the degree of kin interaction in the extended family). If, as Sprey asserts, a corollary to intimacy is an awareness of, and confrontation with, the uniqueness of the other, then certainly marriage must involve a most complex balance of attraction and repulsion, connectedness and separateness, unity and individuality.

All of the sample couples, in one way or another, and in varying degrees, were involved in a continual adaptation to this fact. The most articulate expression of the paradox is however made by Hank, one of the case study husbands:

HANK: I can't imagine not being married to Helen. I think of myself in terms of husband of Helen instead of Hank alone. You know, it's a difficult thing to verbalize. It's more feeling than it is anything concrete. It's a very abstract feeling. . . . I think it's possible to go too far into it or to wake up one morning and to find [that you're] another person or that causes you to say that you've lost yourself and you start evaluating it from a very biased point of view. I never intended to give up my personality. I never wanted to do this. And that frame of mind is broken.

Though he admits that he finds it difficult, Hank's propensity for verbal expression is one reason why he is able to articulate the paradox. More important than this, however, is the fact that for Hank and Helen the paradox is so explicit. Their conflicting conceptions of marriage (open vs. closed) directly touch the issue. Daryl and Debby's conflict over segregated vs. joint conjugal relationships is another relatively explicit illustration of the paradox. And Joe and Jennifer's struggle for domination, more implicit perhaps than in the other case studies, is also a manifestation. (Power struggles may be understood as attempts to both separate and connect. In the sense that the superordinate may perceive the subordinate as different, the struggle is an attempt by each to gain autonomy. In the sense that the superordinate may perceive the subordinate as a dependent, the struggle is an attempt by each to establish a bond.)[3] Finally, Lloyd and Linda's concern over becoming middle class means essentially that they are becoming interdependent on each other. Gone is the independence of their college relationship.

It was not unusual for the sample couples to translate the paradox into spatial management. For some the problem was simply "away time," having moments when one is away from one's spouse.

CHERYL: You know you need outside interests. For instance I don't have many girl friends. I think I need more girl friends. You know there are things you just don't discuss with your husband. You know, not big things but just gossip and things like that. You know, every time I start to gossip he gets mad. I'm a woman and I have these tastes for things he doesn't like. I think we both need friends of our own and ways to be ourselves outside the home away from each other.

INTERVIEWER: Do you [Carl] think it's important that you have male friends?

CARL: Yes I do.

INTERVIEWER: Apart from Cheryl?

CARL: Yes.

For other couples the problem was "alone time," having moments when one is away from one's spouse *and* everyone else.

ALAN: And while she is still napping [after work] that's the time I take a bike ride or sometimes I just get into the car and drive. Sometimes I might go to the beach and look at the water or something like that. That's usually my alone period between four and five or four and six, thereabouts. Then we either have dinner or we go out.

AMY: I think both of us feel the need to be alone on occasion.

What makes "away time" and "alone time" problematic, however, is that each implies, to some degree, a rejection of one's spouse. Each may be interpreted as an attempt *not* to be married. But as Hank points out, not disassociating oneself from one's spouse can destroy a marriage. What it comes down to is that "I-ness" and "we-ness" are both necessary while at the same time incompatible with each other. A recent study of the paradox puts it another way (Askham, 1976). This research (also based on in-depth interviews) sees the problem as the desire on the part of intimates to develop and maintain both a sense of personal identity and interpersonal stability. The author notes that these two activities are essentially contradictory and therefore in potential conflict. The conflict is, however, not only a function of the contradictory nature of "I-ness" and "we-ness." There is also the problem of definition. Just how much autonomy is "too much autonomy" and how much connectedness is "too much connectedness"? For example, although Carl and Cheryl speak of how important it is for them to have outside interests and friends apart from each other, they also believe that one can go too far.

CARL: I think we're probably better off than a lot of the neighbors. I could probably say that most of our neighbors are happily married, but I also think a lot are going in their separate directions. We have a neighbor—she's very women libbed—and they've got a little daughter, her husband just seems to be wrapped up in his work and things like that.

CHERYL: He goes his way and she goes hers.

And Amy believes she must not let her independence get to the point where Alan might begin to feel she doesn't need him.

INTERVIEWER: What do you consider Alan's most important need?

AMY: I think to let him know I love him, and need him. Because I tend to be very independent. I think it's important for him to realize that I need him. As independent as I may sound, he's a big part of my life.

Another reason why the paradox is a source of conflict is that spouses may not always identically define what constitutes "too much." Part of this is due to individuals having different interests and different capabilities for managing the paradox. Hank and Helen, for example, seem to have different definitions of how much is "too much." Similarly, Mark and Marie have disparate attitudes toward their own marital connectedness.

MARIE: He's given all of himself that he can give. He holds back because there's a private part in him that's just him. He likes to be alone, and stuff like that. I think I've given all of myself, because I give everything I can. There's no private part of my life that I keep from him, yet I think he needs a private part of himself.

INTERVIEWER: Is that the way it is, Mark?

MARK: Yeah. It is important for me to be alone, for a while. I'm a little reserved sometimes. I think a lot.

Mark and Marie also have variant capacities to deal with the paradox. Whereas Mark can have a great time by himself, Marie needs people.

MARIE: You're too independent and I'm too dependent.

MARK: No, I depend on you. I depend on you for affection and understanding.

MARIE: You do? Isn't that nice. No, I think he is too independent and I find that I'm too dependent.

INTERVIEWER: What makes you say that he's too independent?

MARIE: Because he is. I think that he could work without anybody else on this whole earth and be happy. I really do. He can go off and do things by himself and have a great time. I can't. I have to have somebody else to share it with or else I don't get any satisfaction out of it.

Finally, spouses may have different capabilities for escape, what may be referred to as different boundaries of the self.

BRAD: I have little yellow bubbles. I can crawl inside and close the door. It's relatively small, going from top of my head to the bottom of my toe, and I can sit all night in the living room with the vacuum going. Barbara's bubble is the size of the house.

FIRST PREGNANCY AND THE MARITAL PARADOX

The anticipated arrival of the child seems to make the paradox more salient. The primary reason is that the child is both a symbol of unity and a symbol of disunity. As a symbol of unity it is viewed (a) as a concrete manifestation of the couple's love for each other,

FRAN: After the baby I think we'll be closer than we are now.

INTERVIEWER: What makes you say that?

FITZ: . . . I feel that the baby is the love that we have for each other, you know?

(b) as a common element on which the couple may focus,

IKE: With the baby we'll have some type of force that will bring us closer to each other. And you never know. A sickness to the baby like a matter of life and death might draw us closer in that respect. There's always something that will crop up that, you know, will keep you, supposedly, hopefully, together.

(c) as a tie that binds the husband and wife to each other,

KEVIN: I think with the child coming along, you have an added responsibility to try and work out the marriage. . . .

KAREN: I think you're right. You feel that with a child you have a responsibility to work it out.

KEVIN: Right, because now you're involving another person, and another life.

(d) as a weapon to keep the husband (or wife?) in tow (connected),

AMY: I think this would be a great weapon with wives over their husbands, when they say, "You don't do as I wish, and I'm going to get a divorce and take that child away from you." I've discussed this with my friend, and she said, "I really have a weapon and I'm going to use it over my husband, because I think he'll do almost anything." And I know how important the child is. And some people use it, and you can see that they do.

Implicit in Amy's remarks is the contention that the wife "owns" the child. Given the results of child custody cases (almost all in favor of the mother), she is not alone in her belief. Ownership, however, involves responsibilities as well as rights. If the child "belongs" to the mother, then she is more likely to "get stuck with it." The fact that it is typically the wife who is tied to the children may explain why only wives in the sample raised the disuniting possibilities of parenthood. Only they, it seems, feared getting so involved with the child that they would be cut off from their spouses. In essence, the child is a symbol of disunity because it reaffirms the separation between male and female roles in our society.

AMY: I think too many times you give up your whole life to your child, and as a result, when the child is three or four or five, or six or seven, he doesn't know how to adjust. I think we too feel a great loss as the child gets older, and is more and more independent. I see this in my mother and father. They just never took a trip or anything. It was always the children first. I think that people who go out once a week, or they'll leave the child with the babysitter, I think it's much better for the child and for the parents.

CHERYL: You know my parents had lived for the kids for so long, done everything with the kids, and I think they were a little out of touch with each other, you know? And this is something I'm very strong about. I'm going to love my children, but the children are going to have to be brought up to realize that I have to be allowed to have time to get away from them. The bedroom door's not always open to the kids.

GLORIA: Once we grew up and left the house, my parents just didn't have it anymore. I don't know what happened, except that my Dad was involved with his work, and my Mom was so involved with our upbringing that they just lost it along the way. Now they're on and off, and they have to learn how to get back. It's kind of sad. I would like to hope that I won't get so wrapped up in my children that I forget what loving is. I don't know how to do it, but I'm going to make a conscientious effort to try.

Conclusion

Conflict theory has traditionally relied on two models of social organization to explain why conflict is ubiquitous

(Duke, 1976: 225-259). The first model, based on a presumed scarcity of resources, is the more popular model. The second model, the organizational necessity model, "presumes the existence of constant and natural tendencies toward increase in the size of social groups and the differentiation of structures and functions within such groups" (p. 257). The fact that a conflict approach to marriage is a seldom used approach may be due in part to the inappropriateness of the claim that these two explanations are the only explanations for why conflict is inherent in a system. It may of course be argued that the "battle of the sexes" is a battle over scarce resources. Since marriage is a transactional system, this would support using the scarcity model to explain marital conflict. But is scarcity a sufficient explanation? I do not think so. Only when the transactional character of marriage is combined with the enslaving and paradoxical nature of the husband-wife relationship does the heuristic value of a conflict approach to marriage become truly apparent.

Thus, how is it possible to claim that contemporary marriage works according to the conflict paradigm? Three reasons: (a) marriage is not a voluntary union and parenthood is not a "freely chosen" life career; (b) marriage is intrinsically related to the broader issue of male-female conflict; (c) marriage is a social relationship in which the paradox of human action (separateness and connectedness) is acute.

NOTES

1. The tri-fold distinction—complementary, independent, joint—is based on Bott's (1971: 53) typology of conjugal roles.

2. The principal social theorist to focus on the paradoxical nature of interpersonal relationships is Simmel (1950); the principal family theorists are Hess and Handel (1959).

3. Raush et al. (1974: 148) define power in a way that emphasizes the paradoxical aspects of the power struggle: "Power can be defined by the (relative) independence of one party from the other and the other's dependence on him for the attainment of goals."

Chapter 7

A CONFLICT APPROACH TO MARRIAGE:

The Problem of Social Order

If conflict is the basic form of marital interaction, how is social order possible? More concretely, how can there be peace in a home when the husband and wife are supposedly out for themselves? To answer these questions, it is important to examine (a) the structure of conflict situations, and (b) the function of power in the marital system.

The Structure of Marital Conflict

Conflicts of interest may be conceptualized as either competitive or cooperative (see Table 1). A classic illustration of competitive conflict is a football game. Since only one team can win, cooperation is not an option. One team's gain (in yardage particularly) yields a corresponding loss for its opponent. Secrecy (e.g., calling plays in the "huddle") and deception (e.g., faking a "handoff") are important to the

TABLE 1
TYPES OF CONFLICT
(after Bernard, 1964; Conn, 1971)

Competition	Cooperation
(1) What one wins the other loses. Cooperative strategies are impossible.	(1) If one wins the other does not automatically lose. Both may win or lose. The conflict is not strictly competitive in the sense that there is at least one possible outcome for which the preferences of the players are not strictly opposed. This does not mean that the compatible outcomes are the most preferred for either side.
(2) Every gain for one contestant yields a corresponding loss for the other contestant. In other words, payoffs for all outcomes are identical; signs are opposite for both players.	(2) Payoffs or values for all outcomes may be different for the contestants rather than identical and reverse signs. In other words, the values of all outcomes may differ for contestants not only in sign but also in magnitude.
(3) Secrecy and deception are paramount.	(3) Strategic use not of secrecy and misleading information—but of precisely the opposite—information convincingly communicated. Having one's strategy found out and appreciated by one's opponent is important.

game's strategy. Labor-management negotiations, on the other hand, typically are cooperative conflicts. Though the rift between the two parties may start as competition, usually in the end (as a result of "talks" and "threats"), a cooperative strategy—an option which is not either side's first choice but which is agreeable to both—is chosen. Ultimately, each side has won a little, and each side has lost a little.

Although some of the specifications of the competitive situation may be present in a marriage, it is unlikely that all of them will be (Bernard, 1964: 701). A husband and wife, for example, may be embroiled in a conflict over whether or not they should buy a new car, but it would be difficult to say with any degree of confidence that the conflict meant the same thing to each (that one person's loss would be interpreted as a corresponding gain for the other). Similarly, although secrecy and deception may sometimes be part of a spouse's strategy, winning in marital conflict more often depends on communicating one's intentions (e.g., "If you buy that car, I'll go on a shopping spree!").

A case in point is the conflict which Fitz and Fran had over Fitz's weekly drinking stint with "the guys." The conflict meant different things to each. As far as Fitz was concerned, his drinking was an avocation. As far as Fran was concerned, Fitz's antics were a personal affront.

FITZ: From the time we were engaged to the time we were married, we didn't see each other that much.

INTERVIEWER: How come?

FITZ: I was over at the guys' all the time. That was one big mistake.

INTERVIEWER: What do you mean, "one big mistake?"

FITZ: I'd go out every night and get smashed like there's no tomorrow.

FRAN: I came second, after the guys.

FITZ: Which I realized was wrong.

FRAN: . . . He just had this thing when we got married, that he had to be with the guys. . . . He was so afraid of losing his friends. . . . I was a lot more prepared for marriage than he was.

FITZ: I was what you'd call a hell raiser before I got married.

FRAN: . . . Even on our honeymoon, he had to play baseball with the guys that Thursday! . . . Now that's a little irregular.

Relying not on secrecy or deception, Fran convinced Fitz to stop his escapades by communicating a threat: If he didn't stop, she would divorce him.

FRAN: From August to almost the following March, or maybe April, I was trying to get him out of the habit of going out. Well, he'd go out and get drunk and come home at 3 or 4 o'clock in the morning. And I'd never know where he was or what he was doing. So it took a while to get him out of that.

INTERVIEWER: How did you get him out of that?

FRAN: I gave him the ultimatum of either stop drinking or I would divorce him, because I couldn't take it any more. I had had it.

INTERVIEWER: So how soon after you were married did you threaten him with divorce?

FITZ: About the first week!

FRAN: No, it wasn't until that next spring.

INTERVIEWER: How long were you married?

FITZ: Six months.

FRAN: Oh no, it was longer than that, about seven or eight.

INTERVIEWER: Did you say, "If you don't stop, I'm going to divorce you?"

FRAN: That's exactly what I said.

And so, because of the limitations of applying the competitive model to the husband-wife relationship, conflicts in the marital system are typically conceptualized as cooperative games (Bernard, 1964: 701). The significance of cooperative conflict is that, unlike competition, it doesn't mean "all out war." Put another way, the cooperative game is a vehicle by which conflicts may be managed and marriage may be preserved. "Both marital and family bonds are, in our culture, of an intimate nature and presumably permanent. Arguments and conflicts of interest are not supposed to destroy or damage such relationships, but must be managed in such a way that whatever solutions are reached can be jointly lived with" (Sprey, 1975: 74).

Managing conflicts is not the same as resolving conflicts. The management of conflicts implies a conflict approach. The resolution of conflicts implies a consensus approach. One way of representing the distinction between these two models is to conceive of a continuum the poles of which would be labeled "pure consensus" and "pure conflict." The area between the two poles is cooperation, a variable. A pure conflict situation is a competitive situation. The difference between cooperation and competition has already been outlined in Table 1. The difference between cooperation and consensus has yet to be discussed. Horowitz, one of the leading proponents of the conflict approach to social life, provides a comparison:

> First: consensus stands for agreement internally, i.e., in terms of shared perspectives, agreements on the rules of association and action, a common set of norms and values. Cooperation for its part makes no demands on role uniformity but upon procedural rules.[1]
>
> Second: consensus is agreement on the content of behavior, while cooperation necessitates agreement only on the form of behavior. We speak of consensus if all members of the Women's Temperance Union agree to abstain from drinking alcoholic beverages. But we speak of cooperation when agreement is reached on the forms allowed for drinking and the forms allowed for curbing the intake of liquor.
>
> Third: cooperation concerns toleration of differences, while consensus demands abolition of these same differences (Horowitz, 1962: 187).

Conflict theory is often criticized for ignoring the role which consensus plays in social interaction. But it is apparent in Horowitz's remarks that conflict theorists do not actually deny the significance of consensus. What they contend essentially is that procedural rules, not values and beliefs (also rules but at a higher level), are the most important consensual abstractions. Correspondingly, when I claim that the fundamental form of marital interaction is conflict, I do not mean that consensus is unimportant in marriage. Rather, I am asserting that the most important consensual abstractions in a marriage (the consensual abstractions on which peace in a marriage is based) are not the values and beliefs of the husband and wife but the procedural rules which they have managed to work out for themselves.

Daryl and Debby's marriage works not because they share a common set of beliefs and values, but because they have been able to establish and maintain a common set of procedural rules (the most important of which is that Daryl will provide the money, and Debby the "care"). Of course, the construction of these rules was not without mishap. In the beginning, for example, Debby was unwilling to devote herself to caring for Daryl. Their conflict over this issue was close to a competitive game simply because Daryl refused to compromise. Debby eventually conceded and the rule became part of their shared world. Their conflict over where to live, on the other hand, is clearly an example of a cooperative game. Daryl insisted that the decision should be his; Debby insisted that the decision should be mutual. The compromise was that the initial decision over whether they should consider buying a particular house would be mutual, but that the final decision over how much to pay would be Daryl's. The cooperative strategy did not mean that their differences had been abolished, only effectively managed. The couple's conflict over Daryl's recreational pattern (play without Debby) was close to a competitive game during the first year of their marriage. It was a game which Daryl was winning. He would go out and play no matter what Debby said. With the onset of the pregnancy and the transition to parenthood, the conflict shifted. Debby had acquired the "weight" to force Daryl into a cooperative strategy. Though she would not be able to get Daryl to completely give up those play activities which excluded her, she would be able to force Daryl into making some concessions.

Joe and Jennifer's relationship was a succession of verbal and physical battles. The violent argument that erupted during the first two years of their marriage was a consequence of their entanglement in an either/or game—either Joe or Jennifer, but not both, could be boss. In an attempt to dislodge themselves from the one-up/one-down situation, they changed to a power structure in which each would be in charge of certain areas. This strategy implies a cooperative game. It was a precarious game because of the difficulty of establishing who would be responsible for what areas and because of the problems inherent in deciding what the value of the respective areas should be.

Hank and Helen's marriage was certainly a compromise arrangement. Their problems began with Helen's negative response to the hypothetical move to Washington, D.C. Her questioning of the value of Hank's educational goals (since it meant possibly leaving New England) could very well have been a "move" to try to get Hank to give up on his aspirations, and to give in to Helen's wish to have a baby. Helen's challenge also served to redefine their relationship as one which approximated more the competitive model (every day without a family being started brought Hank closer to his degree but to Helen it was "just another day wasted"). The situation eventually escalated to the point that a third party, the counselor, was brought in as a mediator. The counselor helped them to manage their conflict by giving them a vocabulary to interpret their situation ("we were just not communicating"). However, this was not as effective as was their eventual compromise—Hank would delay getting his Ph.D. until after the baby arrived, and Helen would delay being a mother until Hank's M.A. graduation.

Lloyd and Linda illustrate that marital conflict need not be perceived by a couple as bad; they regretted what they saw as their "wending toward consensus." Furthermore, they demonstrate that marital conflict may entail more than two "players," a point which has been virtually ignored by researchers (Safilios-Rothschild, 1970). In their situation, Linda's parents (particularly her mother) were sometimes contestants, sometimes Linda's "seconds" in the couple's rather sophisticated battles with each other and with themselves. Finally, perhaps no other couple more clearly showed how in marital games both spouses may lose.

The Politics of Marriage

Implicit in the foregoing argument and in the previous chapter is the supposition that if conflict is the fundamental form of marital interaction, then power—"the ability to affect social life" (Olsen, 1968: 172)[2] —is one of the most important variables in the marital system. Politics—"the total process through which social power is distributed and exercised" (Olsen, 1968: 171)—constitutes the nucleus of the system.[3]

A long-standing debate exists in the marriage and family field over which of two sources of power is primary—ideology or resources (see Bahr, 1972; Blood, 1963; Blood and Wolfe, 1960; Cromwell and Olson, 1975; Heer, 1963a and 1963b; Komarovsky, 1962; Rodman, 1967 and 1972; Safilios-Rothschild, 1970, 1972, and 1976; Scanzoni, 1970). The data here suggest, however, that ideology and resources operate systemically with each other. Furthermore, it seems that a systemic conceptualization of power offers a concrete illustration of how cognitive sociology (e.g., symbolic interaction, phenomenology) and behavioral sociology (e.g., social exchange theory) can be synthesized.[4]

An ideological approach to marital power is based essentially on the assumption that symbol systems not only reflect behavior, they direct behavior.[5] This is, of course, the central axiom in cognitive sociology.

> According to [ideological theory], families do what the culture [the mutually understood and agreed upon symbol system] tells them to do [e.g., patriarchy may be prescribed] (Blood and Wolfe, 1960: 13).

> Language does not simply symbolize a situation or object which is already there in advance; it makes possible the existence or appearance of that situation or object, for it is part of the mechanism whereby that situation or object is created (Mead, 1934: 77-78).

A resource approach to marital power, on the other hand, is based essentially on the assumption that human behavior is directed toward maximizing rewards and minimizing costs. This is, of course, the central axiom in behavioral sociology.

> A resource may be defined as anything that one partner may make available to the other, helping the latter satisfy his needs or attain his goals (Blood and Wolfe, 1960: 12).

Exchange theory assumes that men have needs and that fulfilling these needs constitutes a reward. . . . Social interaction results from the fact that others provide a person's rewards (Singlemann, 1972: 415-416).

The two approaches are not, however, mutually exclusive. Since human beings act symbolically, what is rewarding must be defined (and identified) as such. This not only explains why what we may commonly think of as rewarding (e.g., food, shelter) constitutes a resource, but why companionship, self-esteem, recognition, for example, also reinforce behavior. Paradoxically, the construction and maintenance of symbol systems is determined by the association (in time and space) of certain symbols with certain rewards or costs. The brainwasher, for example, associates certain ideas (symbols) with certain rewards and costs to produce the desired effect. When this dialectical relationship between symbols and exchange is incorporated into a conceptualization of power, the result is a systemic understanding of the politics of marriage (see Figure 1).

The model in Figure 1 depicts marriage as a complex system, open to its environment.

For a given system, the environment is the set of all objects, a change in whose attributes affect the system and also those objects whose attributes are changed by the behavior of the system (Hall and Fagen, 1956: 20).

That a system is *open* means not simply that it engages in interchanges with the environment but that this interchange is *an essential factor* underlying the system's viability . . . the environment is just as basic as the organic system in the intimate system-environment transactions that account for the particular adaptation and evolution of complex systems (Buckley, 1967: 50).

Implicit in the model is the variable, time, and the assumption that the system is emergent—more than the sum of its parts. Symbols and exchange are both components of the

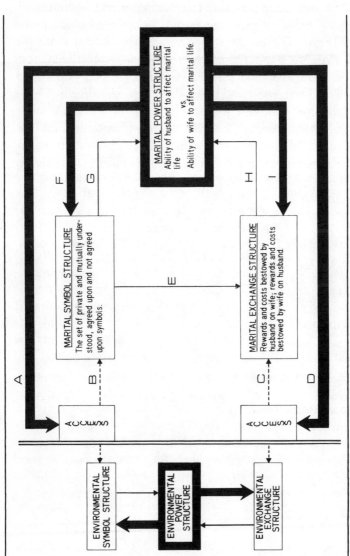

Figure 1. A MODEL OF MARITAL POLITICS

NOTE: The letters in the model do not imply a sequence. They are used so that the various relationships may be referenced. In the text, any reference to a relationship will be denoted parenthetically. For example, (G).

system along with power. Ideology and resources, therefore, conjointly influence and are influenced by the power structure. The interaction among these components is continual. The social order in marriage is thus considered problematic (not a given). The power structure and the output from the power structure are schematically set apart from the symbol and exchange structures and their output (through the use of heavy lines) because the power structure is logically higher than the other components. It is the control center. As such, it is a meta-structural process—it transcends symbols and exchange. The transaction between the system and its socio-cultural environment (which is itself a series of hierarchically structured symbol-power-exchange systems) is denoted by dotted lines.

MARITAL POWER STRUCTURE

The marital power structure is directly based on both the marital symbol structure (G) and the marital exchange structure (H). It, in turn, affects the marital exchange structure (I) and the marital symbol structure (F), which means that it indirectly affects the exchange situation (E). It also affects the system's access to the environment; what symbols are diffused (B), what socio-economic resources are gained and lost by the husband and wife (C) are results of the marital power structure.

Two distinctions are worth noting. The first distinction is between legitimate power and illegitimate power. Legitimate power (sometimes called authority) is used with the consent of the people who are controlled. Illegitimate power is used without the consent of the controlled. An example of legitimate power is provided below. Barbara was "happy" to let Brad be in charge most of the time.

INTERVIEWER: Who would say is in charge? Who makes most of the decisions?

BRAD: I probably make 75 percent of all the decisions.

BARBARA: And I'm very happy about that.

INTERVIEWER: . . . Why did you say you liked the fact that Brad
made all the decisions?

BARBARA: Just what I mean.

BRAD: You don't like the responsibility for the consequences.

BARBARA: I tend to think he is going to come up with a better solu-
tion, so I leave it up to him.

An example of illegitimate power is Daryl's attempt to decide
what house to buy without consulting Debby. It was illegitimate because Debby did not consent to it; she did not like
being told where she was going to live. Legitimate power is
typically the more stable. It is therefore the more desirable—
both to those in power and to those controlled. The trick, of
course, is getting the consent of the controlled. Witness Joe's
attempt to convince Jennifer to accede to him the financial
operations of the marriage.

The second distinction worth noting is between orchestration power and implementation power (Safilios-Rothschild,
1976: 359).[6]

> Spouses who have "orchestration" power have, in fact, the power
> to make only the important and infrequent decisions that do not
> infringe upon their time but that determine the family lifestyle
> and the major characteristics and features of their family. They
> also have the power to relegate unimportant and time-consuming
> decisions to their spouses who can, thus, derive a "feeling of
> power" by implementing those decisions within the limitations
> set by crucial and persuasive decisions made by the powerful
> spouse.

It is not easy to measure the "importance" of decisions.
There is first the "objective" method—measuring importance
by determining which decisions have the most significant
consequences for the couple. "Objectively," such decisions as
what type of job to take, what kind of house to buy, whether
to have a child, etc., all are important decisions (Safilios-
Rothschild, 1969: 297). "Objectively," Daryl was claiming

"orchestration" power when he said, "My presidency of the marriage is in terms of the interface between the inside world and the outside world." He was referring, of course, to his power in the area of deciding where they were going to live. "Objectively," Joe was relegating "implementation" power (and possibly trying to give Jennifer a false sense of power) when he said that she could be "boss for food, shopping, and household decisions." But there is also a "subjective" dimension to "importance." For example, Safilios-Rothschild (1969: 297) suggests that "in-law relations" is not an important area. In the minds of Lloyd and Linda, however, it was very much an important area. Whoever could exert control over how Linda's parents should be perceived (as loving in-laws or as interfering in-laws?) would indeed be wielding orchestration power. The recognition that "importance" is a phenomenological variable also introduces the problem of husbands and wives having conflicting definitions of the situation. For example, a husband may consider a decision so unimportant that he feels there is no need to consult with his wife. His wife, on the other hand, may think the issue too important not to be a joint decision. This kind of situation was implied when Hank talked of how he had been "taking care of" Helen ("By not letting her do it herself—even minor details, say keeping track of the checkbook—I was making rather major decisions with very little consideration for her. Even sometimes without asking her.")

MARITAL SYMBOL STRUCTURE

The marital symbol structure is the phenomenology of the system and it includes all the abstractions (cognitions) of the husband and wife. These abstractions are constructed and maintained directly by the marital power structure (F) and through the system's transaction with the environment (B). The abstractions, in turn, affect the marital power structure— directly by imposing ideological prescriptions (G) (e.g., "The husband should be in charge because the Bible says so."), and indirectly by defining what a resource is (E) and by qualifying the effect of exchange on power (H).[7]

The abstractions may be classified on two dimensions. The first dimension is the degree to which the abstractions are agreed upon or consensual. For example, some goals (a goal is an abstraction) are consensual (both Joe and Jennifer wanted to start a family when they did), other goals are not (whereas Helen wanted a baby after being married for two years, Hank wanted to wait). The second dimension is the degree to which the abstractions are mutually known—the degree to which the husband and wife are both aware of the abstractions in the set. All abstractions which are not mutually known constitute the private or secret worlds of the husband and wife. All abstractions which are mutually known constitute the intersubjective world of the husband and wife. This dimension is by far the more complex of the two—a fact which will become evident through an illustration. When Linda disclosed that she had decided to have a baby to keep Lloyd from quitting his job with her father, she believed she was revealing a secret ("Now it comes out"). Lloyd, however, claimed he was aware of her motive ("No kidding; I knew that"). Thus, although Linda thought her motive was a secret residing in her private world, it was not. It was part of the intersubjective world. Lloyd's knowledge of Linda's motive, however, was a secret residing in his private world. Until he admitted that he knew Linda's motive, Linda was not aware that he knew. The mutuality dimension of Lloyd and Linda's symbol structure before and after Linda's disclosure is diagrammed in Figure 2. Before Linda's disclosure, from Lloyd's point of view, he knew about the motive. He did not know whether Linda knew that he knew (at least he did not say so). Linda's picture of the situation before her disclosure was that her motive was a secret. The real secret was that Lloyd knew the motive. Only he knew that. After Lloyd's disclosure, from Lloyd's point of view, he knew about the motive and he knew that she knew he knew. The secret then moved from the private to the intersubjective world and was no longer

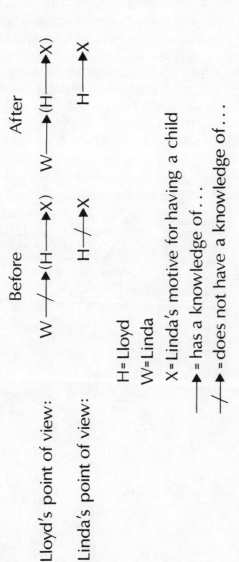

Lloyd's point of view:

	Before	After
	W ⇥̸ (H ⟶ X)	W ⟶ (H ⟶ X)

Linda's point of view:

	Before	After
	H ⇥̸ X	H ⟶ X

H = Lloyd
W = Linda
X = Linda's motive for having a child
⟶ = has a knowledge of . . .
⇥̸ = does not have a knowledge of . . .

Figure 2: MUTUALITY TIME ANALYSIS

NOTE: The complexity of the mutuality dimension is obviously due to its vertical (hierarchical) structure—the familiar phenomenological puzzle (I know that you know, and I know that you know that I know . . . , and so on). For a dis-cussion of the phenomenological puzzle and a means of measuring it in a dyad, see Laing et al. (1966).

a secret. Linda's picture of the situation was the same as Lloyd's. The puzzle can obviously get quite complicated. Imagine the increased complexity with a third party. The point of all this is that knowing where abstractions are located not simply at the present but at particular points in time (knowing the history of the symbol structure) is important for understanding how the system works. A threat, for example, is an idea which has been convincingly transferred, by word or by deed, from the private to the intersubjective world. To really understand the politics of a couple's marriage, it is essential that one know when these transfers are made.

MARITAL EXCHANGE STRUCTURE

The marital exchange structure is the husband-wife reinforcement pattern. It is influenced by the marital power structure (I), by the availability of socioeconomic resources from the environment (C) (e.g., education, income, occupational status), and by the marital symbol structure (E). It, in turn, affects the marital power structure (H). Resource theorists have generally only considered the relative status of the husband and wife's education, income, and occupation (Safilios-Rothschild, 1970 and 1976). In doing so, they have limited their attention to the husband and wife's strategies to gain and block access to environmentally based reinforcements (D). Ignored are the resources which are essentially "internal" to the system and which are influenced directly by the power structure (I). For example, the fact that both Debby and Jennifer lost their socioeconomic independence did not mean that they were powerless. They learned to exploit resources other than those which are derived from the environment. Debby used a "manipulative" strategy ("I always get my way, don't I?"). Jennifer seemed to rely on her wit. The point is that the marital exchange structure is based on more than simply whether or not a spouse has a job. As Safilios-Rothschild (1970: 548) notes:

Does not the wife have at her disposal other "resources" tangible and intangible which she can (and does) contribute or withdraw at will and thus "control" even the most occupationally successful husband? A wife can prepare the husband's favorite dishes or torture him with badly prepared food; can take good care of his clothes or neglect them; keep a neat and attractive house or leave it sloppy and disorganized; be a great companion and host to his guests and colleagues or a miserable one; be a responsive sexual partner or a frigid one, or totally refuse to have sexual relations with him; be sweet, affectionate, understanding, supporting and loving or sour, cold, distant, critical, demanding and unfriendly. . . . Of course, the husband also has at his disposal a similar range of "resources." A husband may share household tasks with his wife or refuse to do anything because of his "heavy" schedule and spend that time drinking with friends; he may go out often with his wife or hardly at all, always disappearing in long meetings, conferences and business trips, even when he is by no means obliged to go to these meetings and trips.

In addition to the effect which the pregnancy had in changing the wives' socioeconomic resources (all but one of the employed wives would not be working after the child arrived), the physical reality of pregnancy also helped to "internally" transform the marital exchange structure. For example, if we accept Safilios-Rothschild's argument that attractiveness and sex may be used as resources, then the fact that a number of husbands and wives talked about how the pregnancy made the wife less desirable would seem to indicate that a wife may lose some of her previously held resources, if only temporarily.

INTERVIEWER: Carl, do you find Cheryl any less desirable?

CHERYL: Be honest!

CARL: Honest? Recently, yes.

INTERVIEWER: How recently?

CARL: I was going to say six weeks. [This sequence took place during the fourth interview, four weeks before the baby was due.]

INTERVIEWER: Cheryl, did you pick that up?

CHERYL: Yes, because I felt less desirable too. When you feel that way it just comes out.

PAM: It's kind of hard to feel sexy when your stomach is out to here.

FITZ: I'm just getting sick of seeing you fat!

FRAN: Me too!

HANK: I don't know perhaps I'm being a little Victorian about it, but it's just a little bit beyond me to make love to a pregnant woman.

GEORGE: Sometimes I feel like I'm with a mother, instead of a wife.

INTERVIEWER: Do you find Nancy just as desirable?

NORMAN: Well, I don't know. She looks pretty good in clothes, and in the dark you can't see, so it's not too bad.

INTERVIEWER: How do you feel about that, Nancy?

NORMAN: She knows it's true.

NANCY: I know.

INTERVIEWER: Do you know how Ike feels?

IRENE: I don't think he's rushing it. Are you, Ike? I don't think he's rushing it. But I don't think he's going through what I did. I think husbands enjoy it, watching it grow.

IKE: It's kind of hard to know what you're enjoying over there.

IRENE: Watching it grow, and knowing it's a miracle.

IKE: I'm really enjoying your big belly. I really am.

IRENE: No, you know, the whole thing, the whole miracle.

IKE: Let's say we tolerate it.

IRENE: Really?!

INTERVIEWER: . . . Are you enjoying it, Ike?

IKE: Yes. You're baiting me with a question, and I don't know. I'm enjoying it to the point where I can enjoy it, and I have no physical feeling on this matter whatsoever, except to watch this phenomenal experiment that reminds me of *Jiffy Pop*. It starts out flat and then pretty soon it's going to burst. Not popcorn is going to come out, but this little—that's my analogy of childbirth right there, for any of your scientific friends. Did you get that on tape, by the way? You can write that in your book!

Also noted by Safilios-Rothschild (1970, 1976) is the assertion that the spouse who feels he/she has relatively more feelings ("love") for his/her spouse than his/her spouse has for him/her will be at a disadvantage in the power struggle. This hypothesis is based essentially on Heer's (1963a) idea that the availability of alternatives (options outside the marriage—e.g., a lover) makes a spouse less dependent on the relationship and more powerful in marital bargaining. Elizabeth, for example, admitted that because of her looks ("Who would want me now?") she began to wonder whether Eric was exploring other sexual options. Assuming the validity of the "relative love involvement" hypothesis, we can speculate that Elizabeth "lost ground" in the politics of her marriage.

ELIZABETH: I really trust Eric a lot, and you have to, because [in his job] he is gone a lot, staying in hotels and stuff, you know, what can you do? You just accept his way of life. But for the first time, once this month, I did question that and asked him about it. Sort of the kind of question, "Can I really trust you?" And I don't think I'd ever really talked about that before, because I hadn't felt the need.

No discussion of power shifts during pregnancy would be complete without some mention of the husbands who see conception as a personal conquest over their wives. It is Elizabeth again who may be the loser when Eric's "old male syndrome" (Me Tarzan, you Jane?) is stirred up.

INTERVIEWER: Eric, do you find Elizabeth any more or less attractive?

ERIC: . . . I find her attractive, as much or more so. It kind of radiates, so-called womanhood, or motherhood.

ELIZABETH: And that appeals to you?

ERIC: Yea. It makes me feel kind of like King Kong.

INTERVIEWER: It makes you feel like King Kong?

ERIC: Yea.

INTERVIEWER: What do you mean by that?

ELIZABETH: Your old male syndrome.

Physical strength is recognized as a resource which all too many husbands use to literally beat their wives into submission. What happens when, because of the physiology of pregnancy, a wife's strength relative to her husband's is even less than before? Joe, who you recall admitted to having used force once "to stop the bad progression of events," also said that Jennifer's lack of "energy" while pregnant prevented her from neglecting the things Joe considered important. Translation: Jennifer was too weak to put up a fight.

JOE: I'm kind of proud of her. More than I was.

INTERVIEWER: What do you mean, "proud of her?"

JOE: She's taking all this in stride. She does pretty well. She seems to listen to me more often than she used to.

JENNIFER: I slowed down, in other words.

JOE: . . . She tries to run the home like a business, and I get very angry at her. . . . She's so involved when she has to do things, she neglects the things I might consider important. But with her pregnancy, she doesn't have the energy, and she is starting to realize it's not all that important.

In anticipation of the couples' postnatal adjustments, I asked who would be responsible for changing the baby's diaper. I got the impression that the husbands would be gaining still another resource. Here was an undesirable chore which they could arbitrarily choose to help with (to reward their wives) or choose not to help with (to punish their wives).

INTERVIEWER: Who is going to be changing the diapers?

IRENE: Uh, he says me. He can't stand messy diapers.

IKE: Well no, uh, don't say it emphatically. I didn't mean it.

IRENE: He has no desire to change the baby.

IKE: I have no outward desire to change diapers, but I probably just out of curiosity would change a diaper. I mean I don't know.

IRENE: I think it would be funny.

INTERVIEWER: Do you have a desire to change diapers, Irene?

IRENE: Uh. . . .

IKE: She likes all those things that go along with motherhood.

IRENE: I have never thought about it. I just knew it was something you had do whether you like it or not.

INTERVIEWER: But Ike has evidently thought about it a little bit more.

IKE: Well, it's not a male role. Let's put it that way.

INTERVIEWER: What do you mean by that?

IKE: Well, you know.

IRENE: It's a mother's job.

IKE: It's a mother's job, you know. Right.

IRENE: No, I don't think I'd mind doing it.

INTERVIEWER: Why do you think Ike is going to mind doing it?

IRENE: I don't think he's going to mind doing it either. Not wet diapers. But a "load." If he knew he had a "load" he might—

IKE: A "load?!" God!

IRENE: He might, you know, ask me to do it, if I was busy or something.

INTERVIEWER: He might ask you if you were busy doing something?

IKE: I'm the reserve diaper changer.

IRENE: Yea, if I was busy doing something and he said, "Oh, the baby is wet," and then he goes to change him or her and then finds out, you know, he might—

IKE: Let's put it this way—I will change the baby only if necessary.

All of the "internal"resource changes illustrated up to now give the expectant husband the advantage. But what about the wife? Does she not gain any resources? Debby epitomizes the wife who can capitalize on being pregnant. She claimed it made her less vulnerable ("I just have the feeling that I can say anything I feel like saying, and nobody dares do anything about it!"). She used it to get out of carrying the laundry ("It was an excuse"). Being exempted from certain chores was not an unusual experience for wives.

AMY: I don't think Alan would have considered doing it [cleaning the tiles in the bathtub] if I weren't pregnant.

GLORIA: I am making more demands on him now, because I tire easily or because I shouldn't be lifting something heavy or that type of thing.

NORMAN: I did little things I'd never done before—haul the laundry down, stuff like that. . . . I don't bother her in the morning. I used to try to get her up to fix my lunch for work, and I don't do it anymore.

And there is the fact that women seem to get more attention when they are pregnant.

AMY: I love being pregnant. I've never gotten so much attention in my life, from Alan and everybody else.

LINDA: It's fun! Everybody does things for you and worries about you. It's nice. . . . I usually don't like attention. I hate to be the center of attraction. But now I'm enjoying it. I don't know why.

The decreased vulnerability, the opportunity to be relieved from the responsibility of household chores, the increased attention—all of these are important changes in the number of resources available to the wife. The question is: Are they enough to balance the losses in the socioeconomic and affective areas? If not, then in terms of the politics of marriage, pregnancy is a losing "campaign" for wives.

Of course, the arrival of the child changes things considerably. The reality of parenthood may, for example, jolt Ike into being more than simply the "reserve diaper changer." Also, with a third party present, coalitions (two against one) are a possibility. Recall in this regard Amy's comments on her friend's use of her child ("You don't do as I wish, and I'm going to get a divorce and take that child away from you.").

Conclusion

How, then, is social order conceivable in a marriage which is a system in conflict? How can there be peace in a home when the husband and wife are supposedly out for themselves? First of all, marital harmony does not require a common value or belief system. A peaceful home need only entail a negotiated management of differences, a cooperative "treaty," which permits the parties to live (however precariously) in spite of their divergent points of view. Second, social order in a marriage is achieved through the legitimate and illegitimate coercion of each spouse by his or her partner. In other words, peace in a marriage, like peace between nations, is a political process.

NOTES

1. Procedure—the set, method, or manner of proceeding in some process or course of action; the way of doing something (Webster, 1958: 1434).

2. There are a number of definitions of power (see Salifios-Rothschild, 1970). The one I am using is relatively broad.

3. Actually all social relationships are power relationships (see Hawley, 1963), and all social relationships are conflict relationships. The issue here is obviously the degree to which conflict and power are salient aspects in a social system. I would argue that the processes are more salient in the husband-wife relationship than in the student-teacher relationship, for example.

4. Rodman's (1967, 1972) cross-cultural data also suggest a systemic approach to marital power. His "Theory of Resources in Cultural Context" recognizes the joint influence of resources on the one hand and of cultural and subcultural differences regarding power on the other. Rodman also notes that a synthesis of these two sources of power brings to the fore the relationship between cognition and behavior (1972: 60).

5. By symbol I mean a conventional sign. "A sign is any cue that has come to stand for something else. . . . Signs may be classified as conventional or natural. A natural sign is a stimulus that is perceived to have a direct [contiguous in time in space] connection with something else for which it becomes a sign. . . . By contrast, the conventional sign derives its meaning from social consensus and can be seen as having a degree of arbitrariness about it" (Kinch, 1973: 57-58).

6. The distinction between these two types of power is also discussed by Komarovsky (1967) and Safilios-Rothschild (1969, 1970).

7. A qualifier or contingent variable is a variable which specifies a relationship between two other variables (Rosenberg, 1968). Rodman (1967, 1972) found that symbols qualify the effect which relative resources have on relative power. The more equalitarian the symbol structure, the stronger the positive relationship between resources and power.

Chapter 8

EPILOGUE

The purpose of this research was to attempt to answer two general questions: How does the husband-wife system work during the first pregnancy? How does the husband-wife system work in general? In answer to the first question, it appears that even before the arrival of the first child, the marital system undergoes shifts in its organization. These shifts are, for the most part, transformations in the type of conflict in the system and alterations in the balance of power. In answer to the second question, the data indicate that the organizational shifts brought on by the transition to parenthood point to the general pattern. That is, marriage works as a system in conflict, and the total process through which social power is distributed and exercised (politics) is the system's nucleus. Although the suggestion that the family is better understood from a conflict rather than a consensus-equilibrium perspective is not new, it is an idea which has been lacking adequate empirical support. This study is, in fact, the first to confront the major assumptions of the conflict perspective "head on." Hopefully, it will not be the last.

In an effort to display the major axioms of the conflict orientation, a model of marital politics was presented (Figure 1). The model depicts the conflict-power process systemically. Its shortcoming is that it illustrates only the existence of relationships. Further research is needed to specify the shape (linear or curvilinear) of the relationships, and the amount of influence (the amount of variation in an independent variable) and time involved (coextensive or sequential) in the relationships (see Burr, 1973: 10-16). The most important addition which the model makes to the argument that marriage is a political process is that it explicitly incorporates the cognitive dimension within the conflict approach. Horowitz (1962: 187) clearly suggests that a conflict approach does not necessarily mean a behavioral approach when he states that while common norms and values may not be important for a social system's stability, a common set of procedural rules most certainly are. Conflict, in other words, does not imply the absence of consensus. Coser (1967: 9), another leading proponent of the conflict framework, recognizes this fact; so does Sprey (1969: 703)—or so it seems. Elsewhere, Sprey (1972: 237) makes a somewhat puzzling statement. He asserts that a conflict approach "implies a framework of exchange." He does not explain what he means by this. If, however, he is saying that cognitive sociology (e.g., symbolic interaction, phenomenology) has no place within a conflict approach, then I must disagree.[1] In my opinion, a more appropriate way of stating the case is that a conflict approach implies a framework of power, and power entails not only the ability to affect reinforcement contingencies (the exchange structure), but also the ability to affect the definition of the situation (the symbol structure). Behavioral and cognitive "theories" are each partial explanations of how marriage (or any sociocultural system) works. In order to achieve a more complete picture, the two "theories" must be synthesized.

While the major limitations of the study are methodological (namely, the "accidental" sampling and the noncollaborative data collection and analysis)[2] some of the major strengths of the study are also methodological. The research is in fact a demonstration of (a) the merits of a qualitative methodology, (b) the advantages of a longitudinal (albeit short-term) design, and (c) the value of a holistic approach. For example, the detection of the importance of the conflict aspect in the couples' marriages was essentially a result of the unstructured interview format and the quasi-inductive mode of analysis. Also, the discovery of organizational shifts during the transition to parenthood was a consequence of the multiple interview design. And as a result of focusing on marriage as a whole (more than the sum of its parts), I was in a better conceptual position to perceive the systemic nature of marital politics. All in all, the study points to the importance of not restricting social science to quantitative techniques, cross-sectional design, and a hypothesis-testing approach.

Perhaps the most significant contribution which this book makes is that it exposes a myth. Marriage and the transition to parenthood are not—indeed cannot be—conflict free. The notion that these experiences are—or could be—void of conflict may, more than anything else, be at the root of dissatisfaction and breakdown in marriage and family systems. We may, in effect, be victims of our own ideals.

NOTES

1. Sprey may of course not be saying anything of the sort. If by a framework of exchange he means the one advanced by Blau (1964) or Thibaut and Kelley (1959), then he is not excluding the cognitive dimension as both of these works attempt to incorporate symbols within an exchange framework.

2. A collaborative approach is essentially a research team approach. The advantages of collaborative interviewing and collaborative analysis are outlined by Laslett and Rapoport (1975).

APPENDIX
DESCRIPTION OF SAMPLE

Table A: Intentions of Couples Toward Conception

Categories	Couples
"Planned" pregnancy	11
Advised off the pill, couple "chooses" to conceive	3
Advised off the pill, couple "unintentionally" conceives (alternative control measures inconsistently employed)	2

Table B: Duration of Couples' Marriages at Conception

Interval	Couples
7 — 12 months	2
13 — 18 months	1
19 — 24 months	3
2 years, 1 month — 2 years, 6 months	1
2 years, 7 months — 3 years	5
3 years, 1 month — 3 years, 6 months	0
3 years, 7 months — 4 years	2
4 years, 1 month — 4 years, 6 months	1
.	
.	
8 years, 7 months — 9 years	1

Table C: Ages of Husbands and Wives at Conception

Husband	Wife
22:0	20:3
22:7	23:1
22:9	20:3
24:4	23:7
24:6	25:0
24:8	23:1
26:2	23:7
26:6	26:0
27:2	26:9
27:5	24:1
27:5	26:8
30:3	26:6
30:10	27:11
31:7	29:11
32:5	25:10
41:7	24:1

NOTE: Tables C, D, E, and F are arranged in ascending order according to the husbands' ages, educations, incomes, and occupations, respectively.

Table D: Educations of Husbands and Wives at Conception

Husband	Wife
Partial high school	High school graduate
High school graduate	Partial high school
High school graduate	High school graduate
High school graduate	High school graduate
Partial college	High school graduate
Partial college	Partial college
Partial college	R.N. diploma
Partial college	R.N. diploma
College graduate	High school graduate
College graduate	Partial graduate school
College graduate	Partial graduate school
College graduate	Graduate degree
Partial graduate school	Partial college
Partial graduate school	R.N. diploma
Partial graduate school	Graduate degree
Graduate degree	Partial college

Table E: Incomes [$] of Husbands and Wives at Conception

Husband	Wife
5,000	0
5,000	9,000
7,000	5,000
7,000	7,000
9,000	0
9,000	7,000
9,000	9,000
9,000	9,000
11,000	500
11,000	5,000
11,000	11,000
15,000	500
15,000	5,000
18,000	11,000
40,000	500
income withheld	income withheld

Table F: Occupations of Husbands and Wives at Conception

Husband	Wife
Graduate student	Professional
Operative	Housewife
Craftsman	Housewife
Craftsman	Housewife
Craftsman	Clerical worker
Craftsman	Professional
Manager	Housewife
Manager	Clerical worker
Manager	Professional (part-time)
Manager	Professional
Professional	College student
Professional	Housewife
Professional	Housewife
Professional	Manager
Professional	Professional
Professional	Professional

REFERENCES

ASKHAM, J. (1976) "Identity and stability within the marriage relationship." *Journal of Marriage and the Family* 38 (August): 535-547.

BAHR, S. J. (1972) "Comment on 'The study of family power structure: a review 1960-1969'." *Journal of Marriage and the Family* 34 (May): 239-243.

BERGER, P. and H. KELLNER (1964) "Marriage and the construction of reality." *Diogenes* 64: 1-25.

BERGER, P. and T. LUCKMANN (1966) *The Social Construction of Reality: A Treatise in the Sociology of Knowledge.* Garden City, N.Y.: Anchor.

BERNARD, J. (1964) "The adjustments of married mates," pp. 675-739 in H. T. Christensen (ed.) *Handbook of Marriage and the Family.* Chicago: Rand McNally.

BLAU, P. M. (1964) *Exchange and Power in Social Life.* New York: John Wiley.

BLOOD, R. O., Jr. (1963) "The measurement and bases of family power: a rejoinder." *Marriage and Family Living* 25 (November): 475-478.

——— and D. M. WOLFE (1960) *Husbands and Wives: The Dynamics of Married Living.* Glencoe, Ill.: Free Press.

BOTT, E. (1971) *Family and Social Network: Roles, Norms, and External Relationships in Ordinary Urban Families.* London: Tavistock.

BUCKLEY, W. (1967) *Sociology and Modern Systems Theory.* Englewood Cliffs, N.J.: Prentice-Hall.

BURR, W. R. (1973) *Theory Construction and the Sociology of the Family.* New York: John Wiley.

CONN, P. H. (1971) *Conflict and Decision Making: An Introduction to Political Science.* New York: Harper and Row.

COSER, L. A. (1967) *Continuities in the Study of Social Conflict.* New York: Free Press.

CROMWELL, R. E. and D. H. OLSON [eds.] (1975) *Power in Families.* Beverly Hills: Sage Publications.

CUBER, J. F. and P. B. HARROFF (1965) *Sex and the Significant Americans.* Baltimore: Penguin.

DEUTSCH, M. and R. M. KRAUSS (1965) *Theories in Social Psychology.* New York: Basic Books.

DUKE, J. T. (1976) *Conflict and Power in Social Life.* Provo, Utah: Brigham Young University Press.

FELDMAN, H. (1974) "Changes in marriage and parenthood: a methodological design," pp. 206-226 in E. Peck and J. Senderowitz (eds.) *Pronatalism: The Myth of Mom and Apple Pie*. New York: Thomas Y. Crowell.

FILSTEAD, W. J. [ed.] (1970) *Qualitative Methodology: Firsthand Involvement with the Social World*. Chicago: Markham.

GARFINKEL, H. (1967) *Studies in Ethnomethodology*. Englewood Cliffs, N.J.: Prentice-Hall.

GLASER, B. G. and A. L. STRAUSS (1967) *The Discovery of Grounded Theory*. Chicago: Aldine.

GOODE, W. J. (1963) *World Revolution and Family Patterns*. New York: Free Press.

HALL, A. D. and R. E. FAGEN (1956) "Definition of a system." *General Systems* 1: 18-28.

HAWLEY, A. (1963) "Community power and urban renewal success." *American Journal of Sociology* 68 (January): 422-431.

HEER, D. M. (1963a) "The measurement and bases of family power: an overview." *Marriage and Family Living* 25 (May): 133-139.

――― (1963b) "Reply." *Marriage and Family Living* 25 (November): 477-478.

HENRY, J. (1965) *Pathways to Madness*. New York: Random House.

HESS, R. D. and G. HANDEL (1959) *Family Worlds*. Chicago: University of Chicago Press.

HILL, R. (1949) *Families Under Stress*. New York: Harper.

HOROWITZ, I. L. (1962) "Consensus, conflict, and cooperation: a sociological inventory." *Social Forces* 41 (December): 177-188.

HOWELL, J. (1973) *Hard Living on Clay Street*. New York: Anchor.

KANTOR, D. and W. LEHR (1975) *Inside the Family*. San Francisco: Jossey-Bass.

KINCH, J. W. (1973) *Social Psychology*. New York: McGraw-Hill.

KOMAROVSKY, M. (1962) *Blue Collar Marriage*. New York: Random House.

LAING, R. D. (1961) *The Self and Others: Further Studies in Sanity and Madness*. London: Tavistock.

―――, H. PHILLIPSON, and A. R. LEE (1966) *Interpersonal Perception*. New York: Springer.

LASLETT, B. and R. RAPOPORT (1975) "Collaborative interviewing and interactive research." *Journal of Marriage and the Family* 37 (November): 968-977.

LEWIS, O. (1959) *Five Families*. New York: Basic Books.

McCORKEL, R. J., Jr. (1964) *Husbands and Pregnancy: An Exploratory Study*. M.A. thesis, University of North Carolina.

MEAD, G. H. (1934) *Mind, Self, and Society from the Standpoint of a Social Behaviorist*. Chicago: University of Chicago Press. (Edited by C. W. Morris.)

MILLER, R. S. (1973) *Pregnancy: The Social Meaning of a Physiological Event*. Ph.D. dissertation, New York University.

OLSEN, M. (1968) *The Process of Social Organization*. New York: Holt, Rinehart and Winston.

OLSON, D. H. (1970) "Marital and family therapy: integrative review and critique." *Journal of Marriage and the Family* 32 (November): 501-538.

――― (1969) "The measurement of family power by self-report and behavioral methods." *Journal of Marriage and the Family* 31 (August): 545-550.

O'NEILL, N. and G. O'NEILL (1972) *Open Marriage*. New York: Avon.

PECK, E. (1971) *The Baby Trap*. New York: Pinnacle.

――― and J. SENDEROWITZ [eds.] (1974) *Pronatalism: The Myth of Mom and Apple Pie*. New York: Crowell.

RAUSH, H. L., W. A. BARRY, R. K. HERTEL, and M. A. SWAIN (1974) *Communication, Conflict, and Marriage*. San Francisco: Jossey-Bass.

RODMAN, H. (1972) "Marital power and the theory of resources in cultural context." *Journal of Comparative Family Studies* 3 (Spring): 50-69.

――― (1967) "Marital power in France, Greece, Yugoslavia, and the United States: a cross-national discussion." *Journal of Marriage and the Family* 29 (May): 320-324.

ROSENBERG, M. (1968) *The Logic of Survey Analysis*. New York: Basic Books.

SAFILIOS-ROTHSCHILD, C. (1976) "A macro- and micro-examination of family power and love: an exchange model." *Journal of Marriage and the Family* 38 (May): 355-362.

――― (1972) "Answer to Stephen J. Bahr's 'Comment on "The study of family power structure: a review 1960-1969"'." *Journal of Marriage and the Family* 34 (May): 245-246.

――― (1970) "The study of family power structure: a review 1960-1969." *Journal of Marriage and the Family* 32 (November): 539-552.

――― (1969) "Family sociology or wives' family sociology? A cross-cultural examination of decision-making." *Journal of Marriage and the Family* 31 (May): 290-301.

SATIR, V. (1964) *Conjoint Family Therapy*. Palo Alto: Science and Behavior.

SCANZONI, J. (1972) *Sexual Bargaining*. Englewood Cliffs, N.J.: Prentice-Hall.

――― (1970) *Opportunity and the Family*. New York: Free Press.

SCHULZ, D. A. (1976) *The Changing Family: Its Function and Future*. Englewood Cliffs, N.J.: Prentice-Hall.

SELLTIZ, C., L. S. WRIGHTSMAN, and S. W. COOK (1976) *Research Methods in Social Relations*. New York: Holt, Rinehart and Winston.

SHIBUTANI, T. (1955) "Reference groups as perspectives." *American Journal of Sociology* 60 (May): 562-569.

SIMMEL, G. (1950) *The Sociology of Georg Simmel*. New York: Free Press. (Translated and edited by K. H. Wolff.)

SINGLEMANN, P. (1972) "Exchange as symbolic interaction: convergences between two theoretical perspectives." *American Sociological Review* 37 (August): 414-424.

SPREY, J. (1975) "Family power and process: toward a conceptual integration," pp. 61-79 in R. E. Cromwell and D. H. Olson (eds.) *Power in Families*. Beverly Hills: Sage Publications.

――― (1972) "Family power structure: a critical comment." *Journal of Marriage and the Family* 34 (May): 235-238.

――― (1971-2) "On the origin of sex roles." *Sociological Focus* 5 (Winter): 1-9.

――― (1971) "On the management of conflict in families." *Journal of Marriage and the Family* 33 (November): 722-732.

――― (1969) "The family as a system in conflict." *Journal of Marriage and the Family* 31 (November): 699-706.

STEINMETZ, S. and M. A. STRAUS [eds.] (1974) *Violence in the Family*. New York: Dodd, Mead.

STEWART, M. and P. ERICKSON (1976) "The sociology of birth: a critical assessment of theory and research." Paper presented at the annual meeting of the Western Social Science Association, Tempe, Arizona, April 29-May 1.

THIBAUT, J. W. and H. H. KELLEY (1959) *The Social Psychology of Groups*. New York: John Wiley.

VIDICH, A. J. (1956) "Methodological problems in the observation of husband-wife interaction." *Marriage and Family Living* 18 (August): 234-239.

VOLKART, E. H. [ed.] (1951) *Social Behavior and Personality: Contributions of W. I. Thomas to Theory and Social Research*. New York: Social Science Research Council.

WATZLAWICK, P., J. BEAVIN, and D. D. JACKSON (1967) *Pragmatics of Human Communication: A Study of Interactional Patterns, Pathologies, and Paradoxes*. New York: W. W. Norton.

Webster's Twentieth Century Dictionary (1958) New York: Publishers' Guild.

WEISS, R. S. (1966) "Alternative approaches in the study of complex situations." *Human Organization* 25 (Fall): 198-206.

WHELAN, E. M. (1975) *A Baby? . . . Maybe*. Indianapolis: Bobbs-Merrill.

AUTHOR INDEX

Askham, J., 118

Bahr, S. J., 132
Berger, P., and Kellner, H., 101 n
Berger, P., and Luckmann, T., 101 n
Bernard, J., 126, 128
Blau, P. M., 151 n
Blood, R. O., Jr., 132
Blood, R. O., and Wolfe, D. M., 41, 82 n, 132
Bott, E., 30 n, 44, 123 n
Buckley, W., 133
Burr, W. R., 150

Conn, P. H., 126
Coser, L. A., 150
Cromwell, R. E., and Olson, D. H., 132
Cuber, J. F., and Harroff, P. B., 19, 43

Deutsch, M., and Krauss, R. M., 88
Duke, J. T., 115, 123

Feldman, H., 19
Filstead, W. J., 30 n

Garfinkel, H., 20
Glaser, B. G., and Strauss, A. L., 30 n, 31 n
Goode, W. M., 115

Hall, A. D., and Fagen, R. E., 133
Hawley, A., 147 n
Heer, D. M., 132, 143
Henry, J., 19

Hess, R. D., and Handel, G., 20, 28, 123 n
Hill, R., 20
Horowitz, I. L., 129, 150
Howell, J., 19

Kantor, D., and Lehr, W., 20
Kinch, J. W., 148 n
Komarovsky, M., 19, 132, 148 n

Laing, R. D., 25, 63
Laing, R. D., Phillipson, H., and Lee, A. R., 139
Laslett, B., and Rapoport, R., 151 n
Lewis, O., 20

McCorkel, R. J., 18
Mead, G. H., 110, 132
Miller, R. S., 18

Olsen, M., 131, 132
Olson, D. H., 30 n
O'Neill, N., and O'Neill, G., 67 n

Peck, E., 108
Peck, E., and Senderowitz, J., 108

Raush, H. L., Barry, W. A., Hertel, R. K., and Swain, M. A., 123 n
Rodman, H., 132, 148 n
Rosenberg, M., 148 n

Safilios-Rothschild, C., 131, 132, 136, 137, 140, 141, 143, 147 n, 148 n

Satir, V., 30 n
Scanzoni, J., 115, 132
Schulz, D. A., 105
Selltiz, C., Wrightsman, L. S., and Cook,
    S. W., 23
Shibutani, T., 95
Simmel, G., 114, 115, 123 n
Singlemann, P., 133
Sprey, J., 29, 64, 104, 105, 108, 114, 116,
    128, 150, 151 n
Steinmetz, S., and Straus, M. A., 82 n
Stewart, M., and Erickson, P., 18

Thibaut, J. W., and Kelley, H. H., 151 n
Thomas, W. I., 49 n

Vidich, A. J., 30 n
Volkart, E. H., 49 n

Watzlawick, P., Beavin, J., and Jackson,
    D. D., 21, 59
Webster's Dictionary, 65, 147 n
Weiss, R. S., 21, 28, 29
Whelan, E. M., 108

SUBJECT INDEX

Abortion, 97
"Alone time," 118-119
Alcohol, 127
Ambition, 90
    and children, 74-75
American Sociologist, 10
Analytical approach in science, 9-12, 20-21
Assertiveness, 62-63, 75-76
Assumptions and action, 58-60
Attention given to pregnant women, 146
Attractiveness during pregnancy, 141-144
Autonomy. *See* Connectedness and Separateness; Individualism
"Away time," 117-118

"Battle of the sexes," 123
Bedtime, 67, 85
Behavioral data and the conjoint interview, 25, 30 n, 60
Behavioral sociology
    and conflict approach, 150
    and systemic conceptualization of power, 132
Bible, 137
Biography reconstruction, 99, 101 n
Birth
    classes, 48
    female's role, 18, 77
    male's role, 17-18, 143-144
Boundaries
    of marriage, 133-135
    of self, 120
Brainwashing, 116, 133
Breadwinning and marital power, 78-81

Case studies, advantages of, 28-29
Chauvinism, 36, 40, 44, 77
Childless couples, attitudes toward, 74, 110, 113
Children
    as basis for marriage, 110
    deciding to have, 33-34, 45, 74-75, 89-90, 94, 108-114, 138, 155
    and divorce, 52, 97, 100, 121
    exploitation of, 45-46, 48-49, 121, 147
    as intruders, 19, 122, 141-143
    and marital paradox, 120-122
    pressure to have, 34, 45, 108-114
    as sanctuary from marriage and work, 109-110
Closed marriage, 67 n
Coalition formation, 147
Cognitive consistency theory, 88, 97
Cognitive organization of behavior. *See* Punctuation
Cognitive sociology
    and conflict approach, 150
    and systemic conceptualization of power, 132, 150
Commitment in marriage, 55-56, 107
Communication
    breakdown, 51-67, 87
    and marital conflict, 126-128
Confidence, 61-62, 75-76, 78
Conflict
    and case studies, 103
    between couples and parents, 83-102, 104
    defined, 104

disclosure of during interviews, 25-26
as good for marriage, 131
between identity and stability, 118-119
between males and females in history, 115-116
resulting from false pregnancy, 57
structure of, 125-131
Conflict in marriage, topics
buying a new car, 126-127
education vs. experience, 77
housework, 36-38, 130
meaning of marriage, 29, 35-36, 38, 41, 45, 54, 55, 58, 66, 117
money, 62, 76, 137
power (explicit discussion), 39, 72-73, 79-81, 131
recreation, 44, 56, 130
school, 131
what is "real," 58-59, 63
what to talk about, 61
when to have a child, 51-67, 131
when to marry, 52
where to live, 38-43, 53-54, 130, 131
who's the expert, 77
work, 37-38, 43, 45, 54, 81-32, 115
Conflict management vs. conflict resolution, 64, 128
Conjoint interviews
advantages of, 25, 30 n, 60
as clinical tool, 30 n
as three-person system, 67
Conjugal role segregation, 44, 45, 104
Connectedness and separateness
and ambivalence in marriage, 113
and bedtime, 67, 85
and children, 74
and friends, 96
and marital paradox, 116-120
and meaning of marriage, 54-55
and middle-class way of life, 84-85, 89
and parents of couples, 84-85
and power, 117
and recreation, 44, 56, 130
and work, 53
Constant comparative method, 30 n
Contingent variable defined, 148 n
Contraception, 18, 155
Contradiction between thought and behavior, 60, 83-101, 104

Cooperation
and competition, 126
and consensus, 64, 129
Counseling, 51, 57, 58, 62, 92, 131
Crisis
defined, 33, 49 n
and first pregnancy, 19
as medium to study social systems, 20

Deception
and marital symbol structure, 138
and multiple interviews, 25-26
and parents of couples, 86
and structure of marital conflict, 125-127
Dependency, 59, 61, 96, 117
Diapers, 48, 144-145, 147
Disconfirmation defined and illustrated, 59-63
Divorce, 52, 55, 57, 64, 107-108
and children, 97, 121, 147
as personal weakness, 70
rate, 105

Either/or game, 130
Emergence, principle of, 20-21, 133, 151
Empirical evidence
and conflict approach, 29
and qualitative research, 11
and quantitative research, 11-12
"Empty nest syndrome," 122
Engagement ring, 86, 100
Environment of a system defined, 133
Environmental exchange structure, 134
Environmental power structure, 134
Environment symbol structure, 134
Equalitarianism, 115-116, 148 n
Ethnomethodology, 20
Exchange theory, 132-133, 151 n
Expectant fathers, researchers' implied attitudes toward, 18
Extended family, 116
Extramarital sex, 143

False pregnancy, 26, 57
Familism, 54-55, 65, 75
Feedback system, 59, 61, 133-135
Free time. See "Alone time"; "Away time"; Connectedness and Separateness

Friends
    and organization of marriage, 28
    and transition to parenthood, 34, 45,
        95, 111

Game theory, 125-131
"Generalized other," 110
Gifts, their effect on marriage, 87-89, 91-
    93, 97, 99
Guerilla tactics, 48
Guns in the home, 80

Help from husbands during pregnancy,
    146
Holistic approach in science, 9-12, 20-21,
    151
Home
    and middle-class way of life, 89
    and decision to have a child, 90
Honeymoon, 127
Housework, 36-38, 43, 45, 46-47, 80, 141,
    146
Hypothesis testing, 21, 29, 151

Ideological theory of marital power, 40-
    41, 81, 82 n, 132-133, 137
Ignoring one's spouse. See Disconfirma-
    tion
In-depth interviews, advantages of, 19,
    24-25, 151
Independence, 71-75
Individualism
    and apartment living, 89
    and familism, 54-55
    and marriage, 87, 94, 116-120
    and middle-class way of life, 84
Industrialization and marriage, 115-116
"I-ness" and "we-ness," 118-119
In-laws. See Parents of couples
Instrumental learning theory, 88
Interactional cycle, 59-62
Intersubjectivity, 25, 39, 81, 138. See also
    Marital symbol structure
Introversion, 59-62

"Keeping up with the Joneses" and chil-
    dren, 111-112

Labeling, 39-43, 49 n, 131
Language and "reality" construction, 132

Living together unmarried, 83, 106-108
Longitudinal research, 25-26, 28, 151
Losing in marital games, 131
Lying. See Deception

Manipulation, 36, 37, 41-42, 48, 140
Marital exchange structure, 134, 135, 140-
    147
Marital paradox, and first pregnancy, 120-
    122
Marital politics, model of, 134-150
Marital power structure, 134, 135, 135-137,
    140
Marital symbol structure, 134, 135, 137-
    140
Marriage
    ambivalence in, 112-113
    as bondage, 108
    companionship type, 19
    decision to marry, 61, 70, 105
    as emergent system, 20-21
    inside vs. outside, 42
    vs. living together, 106-108
    as negotiated order, 64, 73
    as neolocal unit, 116
    as open system, 114-116, 133, 134
    organization of, 28-29
    as paradox, 116-123
    as permanent relationship, 107-108,
        128
    popular perceptions of, 29, 151
    as precarious order, 135, 147
    as private world, 20
    vs. single life, 105-106
    as slavery, 108
    as transactional system, 114-116, 133-
        134
    compared to world affairs, 147
Methodology
    acceptance rate, 23, 30 n
    analysis, 27, 30 n, 67
    constant comparative method, 30 n
    data collection, 20, 21-27
    interviews, 24-27, 30 n, 150-151
    problems of entry and trust, 20, 21-23
    sampling procedure, 22-23, 150
Middle-class way of life, 83, 84, 87
Military, 52, 54
Money and structure of marriage, 52, 55,
    62, 87-89, 91-93, 97

Modernization, 115-116
Multiple interviews, advantages of, 25-26
Mutuality, 25, 138-139
Myths about marriage, 151

Nagging, 59
Neolocal family, 116
Nepotism, 85, 91, 93, 97-99
     and deciding to have a child, 94, 138
Normalization (defining the atypical as
     routine), 46-47

Obstetricians' role in study, 20, 21-23
One-up/one-down situation, 130
Open marriage, 67 n, 133

Paradox in marriage, 116-122
Parenthood
     exploitation of, 45-46
     as trap, 114
     as wife's domain, 18, 48, 80, 145
Parents of couples, 28-29
     and fear, 93
     as intruders, 88, 91, 92, 98
     as negative referents, 84-85, 94
     and orchestration power, 137
     as players in marital games, 131
Patriarchy, 42, 71, 82, 115-116
Phenomenological theory, 132, 150
Physical force. See Violence
Politics
     defined, 131-132
     of marriage, 131-147
     as nucleus of marital system, 132
Popcorn as a metaphor to describe preg-
     nant women, 143
Power defined, 123 n, 131, 147 n
Power in marriage. See also Marital power
     structure
     "behind the scenes," 42
     and connectedness and separateness,
          117
     formal vs. informal, 42
     importance of, 131
     as a meta-structural process, 135
     legitimate vs. illegitimate, 135-136
     orchestration vs. implementation, 136-
          137
     problems of measurement, 136-137
Procedural rules and marital conflict, 64,
     129, 147 n, 150

Pregnancy
     as crisis, 33-34
     exploitation of, 46-48, 130, 146
     before marriage, 18, 111
     as personal conquest, 143-144
     as medium to study marriage, 20, 30 n
     physical reality of, 26-27, 46-47
     psycho-social reality of, 26
Pressure
     to have child, 34, 45, 108-114
     to marry, 86-87, 105-108
Pronatalism. See Pressure to have a child
Punctuation of interactional cycle, 59, 61

Qualifier variable defined, 148 n
Qualitative research, 19
     analysis, 27, 30 n
     and conflict and power in marriage,
          151
     data collection, 24-27
     defined, 30 n
     and theory generation, 31 n
     and holistic research, 9-12
Quickening, 26

Reasons for couples, participation, 23-24
Recreation, 35, 38, 43, 44, 49, 56, 67,
     85, 94, 95
Reference groups,
     and deciding to have child, 34, 110-
          112
     defined, 95
     and labeling, 96
Rejection defined, 59
Relative deprivation and deciding to have
     a child, 111-112
Relative love involvement hypothesis, 143
Religion, 70, 75, 106, 137
Resources defined, 41, 132. See also Mari-
     tal exchange structure
Resources in a cultural contex and marital
     power, 148 n
Resource theory of marital power, 41,
     82 n, 78, 132-133
Resources, types of,
     ability to conceive child, 143
     attractiveness, 141
     availability of alternatives, 143
     children, 45-46, 121, 147
     companionship, 141

competency, 40-43, 45
housework, 141
internal vs. external, 140
money, 45, 78, 79, 81
parenthood, 45-46, 130
pregnancy, 46-48, 130, 146
recreation, 141
relative love involvement, 143
sex, 141, 143
socio-economic, 140
strength, 82 n, 144
violence, 82 n, 144
wit, 140
work, 69, 78-79, 140-141
Retrogression defined, 86
Roles, ascribed vs. achieved, 115
Routine grounds of everyday life, 20

Sample description, 23, 31 n, 155-157
School
and deciding to have a child, 74
and familism, 55, 65
and marital conflict, 53
and middle-class way of life, 86, 89
Science, approaches in, 9-12, 20-21, 151
Secrecy. See Deception
Self-report data and the conjoint interview, 25
Sex during pregnancy, 141-144
Sex roles, 181, 19, 78, 82, 96, 115-116, 145
Single life, 105
Socialization
and ambition, 91
and marital power, 35-36, 71
in middle class, 86
and military, 54
and reaction to cohabitation, 106
of women, 116
Social relationships as power relationships, 147 n

Spatial management, 117-120. See also Territoriality
Stages of pregnancy, 18, 26-27
Student movement, 83, 91, 95
Symbols, 132, 148 n. See also Marital symbol structure
Symbolic interaction theory, 132-150
Subordination, 59, 61, 62, 63, 116. See also Power

Temper tantrum, 72
Territoriality, 92-93, 101. See also Spatial management
Theory, generation of, 30, 31 n
Threats, importance of, 126-128, 140
Time as variable in marital system, 133, 139-140
Treaties in marriage, 147

Ultimatums. See threats
Unemployment during pregnancy, 64
Utilitarian marriage, 43

Violence, 71-73, 80, 82, 82 n, 130, 144

War metaphor, 38, 128, 147
Withdrawal, 59
Work
and connectedness and separateness, 53
and deciding to have child, 74-75, 94, 138
and familism, 54-55, 65, 75
and housework, 37-38, 79-81
and marital conflict, 37-38, 43, 45, 54, 81-82, 115
and marital power, 69-82, 140-141
and the organization of marriage, 28
and self-concept, 75-76, 99
and transition to parenthood, 18, 64, 66, 78, 81-82, 100-101, 114, 141

ABOUT THE AUTHOR

RALPH LaROSSA was born and raised in New York City. He received his B.S. from St. Peter's College, his M.A. from the New School for Social Research, and his Ph.D. from the University of New Hampshire. He is currently Assistant Professor of Sociology at Georgia State University in Atlanta and is involved in continued research on marital conflict and the transition to parenthood.

NOTES

NOTES

NOTES